Blessed Assurance

D1245433

Foundational Truths for the Christian Life

By
Jim Binney, D.Min

The Counselor's Pen Publications
Greenville, SC

Table of Contents

✿ ✿ Preface ✿ ✿

Having pastored for over seventeen years, I have witnessed the heart-wrenching sight of seeing a new convert, excited in his new-found faith, fall by the wayside in defeat and frustration … another casualty in the ongoing war between the forces of God and Satan. "Why does this happen?" I asked myself, "and why does it happen so often?"

Thus the burden for this book was placed upon my heart. For some years I struggled with the formidable task ahead of me. I excused myself from it with the overworked justifications of personal inadequacy, lack of time and the "Surely someone else will do it" cliché. But God wanted me to do it.

I am strongly convinced that the new believer "hungers and thirsts for righteousness" immediately following salvation more than at any other time of his Christian experience! This truth is implied, if not stated, in the first epistle of Peter, *"As newborn babes, desire the sincere milk of the word, that ye may grow thereby." (1 Peter 2:2).*

The key word in this verse is DESIRE. A newly born-again Christian is a spiritual babe; and just as a little infant desires milk to satisfy his hunger, the "newborn babe" in Christ has a "desire" for the "milk of the word!" I believe that Peter is giving a *description* of the new Christian as well as a *command* to the new Christian. He is simply saying that the new believer has an unprecedented desire for the Word of God which is proper as well as timely! A key reason for introducing the new Christian to the "first principles" immediately following his salvation is because of his God-given "hunger and thirst."

BLESSED ASSURANCE

The most vital of all these "first principles" is the grand and glorious truth of the certainty of our salvation, what the Bible describes as *"everlasting life"* and *"eternal life."* It is a theme which is woven through the tapestry of God's Word. Like a thread of gold in the hem of a queen's garment, it glistens and glimmers and adorns the whole. In fact, one entire book of the New Testament is devoted to the truth of the absolute assurance of our eternal life. The Apostle John wrote *"These things have I written unto you that believe on the name of the Son of God; **that ye may know that ye have eternal life**..." (1 John 5:13). [Emphasis added]*

The burden of my heart is to place this book into the hands of the new convert as a tool to guide him through this all-important stage of his Christian life. It could be used as a classroom text in a "new converts" setting, with a fellow Christian in a one-on-one training situation, or even for personal use by the new believer in the privacy of his own home if the above opportunities are not available. It is my sincere desire and prayer that God would be pleased to use this book to help you, dear reader, to enter into a new life with our blessed Lord. May you grow to love Him and serve Him with all your heart!

Jim Binney

Blessed Assurance

Blessed assurance, Jesus is mine.

O what a foretaste of glory divine!

Heir of salvation, purchase of God,

Born of His Spirit, washed in His blood.

Perfect submission, perfect delight,

Visions of rapture now burst on my sight;

Angels descending, bring from above

Echoes of mercy, whispers of love.

Perfect submission, all is at rest,

I in my Savior am happy and blest;

Watching and waiting, looking above,

Filled with His goodness, lost in His love.

Chorus:

This is my story, this is my song,

Praising my Savior all the day long;

This is my story, this is my song,

Praising my Savior all the day long.

$\wp$ $\wp$ *Chapter One* $\preceq$ $\preceq$

"What Happened to Me?!"

*These things have I written unto you that believe on the
name of the Son of God; that ye may know that ye have
eternal life, and that ye may believe on the name of the
Son of God.   (1 John 5:13)*

"Brudder Binney! What happened to me? I feel all funny
inside of me!" Joey, who had just been saved, blurted out this
question.   Only a few minutes had elapsed since this eight-year-
old boy had asked Christ to save him while sitting on a log beside
a lake at Camp Civitan.   I never saw a convert so excited about his
new-found faith as was little Joey! He ran off telling everyone
who would listen how God had saved him.   That night following
the chapel service, he eagerly came forward after the sermon to
make a public stand for Christ.

The next night after the sermon he came forward again and
was dealt with by another counselor.   The same thing happened
the next night and the next! I sought out Joey to learn why he kept
coming forward at the invitation.   When I found him and asked
him, he replied, "Oh, Brudder Binney, I ain't never felt so good in
my life! I wanna do it again every chance I get!" Although little
Joey did not understand that it is only necessary to pray once to be
saved, he understood the joy and peace that is found in Christ.

Perhaps you have wondered the same thing Joey has: "What has happened to me?" Assuredly something marvelous and exciting has happened to you! To help you understand what has happened, we will cover two major truths in this chapter: *What you did* and *What you have as a result of your new life in Christ Jesus.*

WHAT YOU DID

You Acknowledged Your Sinful Condition

You have accomplished one of the most difficult things known to the human mind. Many others have not been able to do what you have done. You have acknowledged your sinful condition. You have admitted that you are a sinner. This is not an easy thing to do, but it is absolutely necessary for one to be saved. *"For all have sinned, and come short of the glory of God."* *(Romans 3:23).*

This is a clear teaching of the Bible, but it still remains one of life's most difficult admissions. Man wants to see himself in the best possible light. We do all we can to cover over our sins with works of righteousness, and yet, God says, *"... all our righteousnessses are as filthy rags." (Isaiah 64:6).*

Some years ago, a young Marine attended the services of our church. I preached a message that morning on the sinful, depraved condition of mankind. I stressed that we are all sinners, that there is none righteous, that all we like sheep have gone astray. After the service, he came to me as I stood at the door and stiffly declared, "I don't think you should have preached that way in your sermon! You left the impression that everybody is full of

2

sin. I believe that there is some good in everyone. It would have been better to have emphasized that rather than the evil."

This young man's problem was based on the popular misconception of man's so-called goodness. He had not yet come to the place where he could admit that without Christ, man is hopelessly sinful and eternally lost.

God, in His marvelous grace, has revealed our lost condition to us. He revealed this to a little boy named Joey, and He has revealed the same to you. For this, you should ever be thankful because without this realization, you would never have asked for God's help. You have taken this important step. You have acknowledged your sinful condition.

You Acknowledged Your Need Of Salvation

You have also acknowledged your need of salvation. The first step in your salvation was to admit you are a sinner. The next step was to admit you really and sincerely needed to be saved.

As a young man still in college, I worked two summers at a camp in South Carolina. It was a special place used for the underprivileged, inner-city kids of that area. It was my job to teach a boating class in the lake located nearby. Of course, I had to insure that all the boys in my class could swim before they ventured onto the water. After they all declared their outstanding ability as world-class swimmers, I gave them a simple test to satisfy my requirement. I stood upon a diving platform a few yards from the boating dock with a ring buoy in my hand. They were to jump into the water, swim to my platform, tread water and on, my signal, return to the boat dock.

All went well until it came to Pete's turn to take the plunge. I could see that he was a bit apprehensive as he stared into the water. "Pete," I called, "are you sure that you know how to swim?" "Sure," he replied with a slight tremor in his voice. With a look of pathetic sadness, he leaped into the water. Immediately, I could see a problem! With arms thrashing wildly, mouth wide open, and eyes the size of saucers, he churned the water into a froth! His head and shoulders were clear of the surface of the water through the sheer force of his struggles, and yet, he was going nowhere.

The other boys on the dock called his name, but he couldn't hear! One of them started to jump in to rescue his friend, but I warned him away. I threw a ring buoy to Pete. It landed directly in front of his face, but his hands were thrashing on either side of it without touching it! I quickly pulled it in and once again threw it to him. This time the buoy fell behind him with the rope lying across his shoulder. But in his state of panic, Pete could not see it. I leaped into the water! With the cries of alarm of the boys mixed with the pitiful screams of the drowning Pete, I made my way to him and pulled him to shore. Afterwards on the beach, I asked him, "Why didn't you tell me you couldn't swim!" "If I had told you that," he answered, "I couldn't have been in the boating class!"

Pete was operating under the delusion that he could make it on his own. He knew that he couldn't swim, but he hoped that by jumping in anyway, he could make it to the diving pier somehow and still get in on the fun! But, he was wise enough, once he was aware of the seriousness of his predicament, to call out for help. You have done the same thing. You knew you were a sinner, and you called out to the only Person Who could save you … Jesus. You realized that others couldn't save you. You also knew that you could not save yourself.

How tragic that so many people today insist that they can make it to heaven on their own. They don't realize that the Scriptures are emphatic when they declare: *"For by grace are ye saved through faith; and that not of yourselves: it is the gift of God: Not of works, lest any man should boast." (Ephesians 2:8-9).*

The sad truth is that men enjoy boasting about their rightful place in Heaven, after they indignantly assert, "my good outweighs my bad, so God will have to let me in!" The Lord Jesus refers to people like this in His famous Sermon on the Mount: *"Many will say to me in that day, Lord, Lord, have we not prophesied in thy name? and in thy name have cast out devils? and in thy name done many wonderful works? And then will I profess unto them, I never knew you: depart from me, ye that work iniquity." (Matthew 7:22-23).*

Notice what they are trusting in … their witnessing, their wonders, and their works … and yet none of these things are enough to save them.

What then *is* needed? As Pete needed a lifeguard, you needed salvation. Jesus said, *"I am THE way, THE truth, and THE life: no man cometh unto the Father, but by me." (John 14:6).* [Emphasis added]

Between a Holy God and sinful man there is a great gulf fixed. Man has attempted in vain to span that gulf for centuries with his own works and his own efforts, not realizing that the only answer is Jesus.

But you acknowledged your sinful condition. Then you acknowledged your need of salvation, and lastly, you realized that salvation comes only through Jesus Christ.

You Acknowledged Christ As Your Saviour

There is much confusion abroad concerning the vital difference between true salvation and false salvation. Many are the people who believe that the only thing necessary for salvation is to believe in God. But the difference between mental belief for the sake of information and spiritual belief for salvation is the difference between life and death.

The word "believe" in the Bible has more than one meaning, and this fact may contribute somewhat to the confusion. For example, James declares that the devils believe in God. *"Thou believest that there is one God; thou doest well: the devils also believe, and tremble." (James 2:19).*

Certainly, the devils are not going to Heaven, but what is the explanation? Wuest informs us that "believe" in this passage means to "give credence to,"[1] or in other words, to give assent to a fact. The devils admit to the existence of God, but that does not save them. Theirs is merely a mental belief.

On the other hand, Paul informs us of the importance of believing in a spiritual way. *"That if thou shalt ... believe in thine heart that God hath raised him from the dead, thou shalt be saved.*

6

For with the heart man believeth unto righteousness." (Romans 10:9-10).

Belief must travel only a few inches to enable one to be saved: from the head to the heart.

Paul uses "believe" in a different sense than James did. His meaning is "to place one's confidence in, to trust, signifies reliance upon, not mere credence."[2] The belief of the devils is to give assent to a fact, to give credence to the existence of God. The belief of Paul, on the other hand, is one of trust. What you did, dear friend, was to go beyond a mental belief in the mere existence of God to a trust in God's Son for salvation.

Some time ago an amazing true incident occurred to illustrate this truth. A crowd had gathered at the famous Niagara Falls to observe an amazing feat. A world famous tightrope walker was about to walk across a rope which was stretched across the deadly falls from one shore to another. If that were not unusual enough, he was going to push a wheelbarrow ahead of him. With bated breath, the crowd watched in hushed silence as the man began his death-defying journey.

Slowly he placed one foot in front of another as he steadily crept across the slippery, narrow path of rope. He reached the other side amidst the resounding cheers of the awaiting crowd. As he looked victoriously over the spectators, his eye was attracted to one in particular. This man was vigorously leading the cheers of the entire multitude for the hero of the hour. The tightrope walker approached this fan and interrupted his self-appointed cheerleading. "Sir," he said. "Do you believe I can do that again?" "Of course I do," he replied. "I believe it more than I believe anything!" Whereupon the daredevil balanced himself and his wheelbarrow upon the rope, turned to the man and said, "Well then ... climb into the wheelbarrow!" The outspoken man stood embarrassed and chagrined when he realized the difference between belief and trust. And the difference between you and the man who is lost today is that you have climbed into the wheelbarrow of trust. You have followed Paul's admonition to the Philippian jailor to *"Believe* (trust) *on the Lord Jesus Christ, and thou shalt be saved." (Acts 16:31).*

You admitted your sinful condition, you confessed your need of salvation and then, most importantly, you came to the one Person who could save you ... the precious Lord Jesus Christ.

We have considered what you did; now we turn our attention to ...

WHAT YOU HAVE

The Gift Of Eternal Life

"For the wages of sin is death; but the gift of God is eternal life through Jesus Christ our Lord." (Romans 6:23). According to this passage of scripture, you are the proud possessor of a great and marvelous "gift"... the gift of eternal life. Please notice that this is not a purchase nor is it a reward. You cannot buy salvation and you cannot do anything tos deserve it. If you could do either, it would cease to be a gift. If you could buy it, it would be a purchase; if you could deserve it, it would be a reward. It would no longer depend on the love of the giver but the merit of the receiver. God wants to make it very clear that eternal life is

not something for which we are responsible. *"God so loved that he gave ..."* That is the message of salvation. Salvation is *"Not by works of righteousness which we have done, but according to his mercy he saved us."* *(Titus 3:5).*

Joy

There is something else that you have and that is joy. David refers to *"the joy of thy salvation." (Psalm 51:12).* It should be understood that joy is different from happiness in several ways. Happiness is dependent upon circumstances. Thus, if someone has bad circumstances, he is described as "hapless", and if he is full of good circumstances, he is said to be "happy" and if something occurs by chance, it is said to "happen". So then happiness comes from the outside from that over which we have no control.

Happiness has been compared to a thermometer. A thermometer reacts to the environment and reflects it to the observer. Joy, on the other hand, is more akin to a thermostat because it is constant and it controls the environment. Happiness comes from without and can be obtained by anyone. A new car, a raise in pay, or good news can produce happiness. Joy comes from within and can be produced only by the Holy Spirit. Joy may be dormant, but it never leaves us entirely because it is a product of the Holy Spirit and thus the writer has recorded: *"... Weeping may endure for a night, but joy cometh in the morning." (Psalm 30:5).* This is the reason that a child of God can bury a loved one and still smile through his tears. Don't expect always to have effusive feelings of happiness because there will be times of sorrow and weeping. Even our Lord was described as *"... a man of sorrows, and acquainted with grief." (Isaiah 53:3).* There will be trying times in your life as a Christian, but the Spirit of God is within you with generous portions of joy. That is what you have as a Christian and the world knows nothing about it. So you see, you now have a gift which is accompanied with joy, but you also have ... *"peace that passeth understanding." (Philippians 4:7).*

Peace

Source of Peace

Oh, how the world longs for peace. The world creates elaborate organizations such as the United Nations to ensure peace among men. But the wars and rumors of wars march on without respite. I am reminded of the sad words of Longfellow when he wrote:

> And in despair I bowed by head
> There is no peace on earth I said,
> For hate is strong
> And mocks the song
> Of peace on earth, good will toward men.
>
> Taken from *"Christmas Bells"* by Henry Wadsworth Longfellow

Whether it be a nation or an individual, it is difficult to admit that we, in our progressive, scientific age, cannot produce peace. "But," we are told, "there is a solution to this! ... simply refuse to admit it and loudly proclaim that peace is your possession!" I see this "ostrich-in-the-sand" mentality everywhere I turn. In fact, I practiced it myself before I was saved. How sad this is when we realize that so much of this peace is not peace at all. The prophet Jeremiah describes this type of person saying, *"Peace, peace; when there is no peace." (Jeremiah 6:14).*

How different are the people who have come to the "Prince of Peace," the Lord Jesus Christ. *"Peace I leave with you, my peace I give unto you: not as the world giveth, give I unto you. Let not your heart be troubled, neither let it be afraid." (John 14:27).*

Christ's peace is not the peace of the world. The peace we find in Jesus is not the peace the world can understand, nor can it be found in the world. As the song goes:

> There's a peace in my heart that the world never gave,
> A peace it can not take away;
> Tho' the trials of life may surround like a cloud,
> I've a peace that has come there to stay!
>
> Taken from *"Constantly Abiding"* by Anne S. Murphy

That is why it is a *"peace that passeth understanding."* You, dear Christian friend, have received that peace. How thankful you should be! And what is the result of this wonderful peace? *"And the peace of God, which passeth all understanding, shall keep your hearts and minds through Christ Jesus." (Philippians 4:7).*

Result of Peace: Stability

Why is this peace so necessary for the Christian? Paul

tells us that it keeps our hearts and minds. One of the reasons we must understand the importance of the full assurance of salvation is because it brings peace ... and peace brings stability. Without assurance you will not have peace, and without peace you will not experience a heart and mind that is kept in Christ Jesus.

Joey understood the thrill of his salvation, although he did not understand that salvation is not something to be sought after night after night, but that the life in Christ is ... ETERNAL LIFE.

"For God so loved the world, that he gave his only begotten Son, that whosoever believeth in him should not perish, but have EVERLASTING LIFE" (John 3:16) [Emphasis added]

"He that believeth on the Son hath EVERLASTNG LIFE." (John 3:36) [Emphasis added]

"Verily, verily, I say unto you, He that heareth my word, and believeth on him that sent me, hath EVERLASTNG LIFE, and shall not come into condemnation; but is passed from death unto life." (John 5:24) [Emphasis added]

"And this is the will of him that sent me, that every one which seeth the Son, and believeth on him, may have EVERLASTNG LIFE." (John 6:40) [Emphasis added]

"Verily, verily, I say unto you, He that believeth on me hath EVERLASTING LIFE." (John 6:47) [Emphasis added]

"My sheep hear my voice, and I know them, and they follow me: And I give unto them ETERNAL LIFE; and they shall never perish." (John 10:27-28) [Emphasis added]

All these scriptures are the very words of our Lord Jesus Christ. They came from His heart, through His lips, and have echoed loudly and clearly down through the centuries. Some have tried to minimize them and deny them, but God's Word is clear about such people. *"If any man ... consent not to ... the words of our Lord Jesus Christ ... He is proud, knowing nothing."* *(1Timothy 6:3-4).*

Paul warns us about the people who would defame the testimony of Christ, and he warns us that we should "withdraw" ourselves from them. Why is such importance attached to the words of Jesus? Because *"the words that I speak unto you, they are spirit, and they are life."* *(John 6:63).*

The words written above, spoken by Christ regarding "eternal life" and "everlasting life," demand our utmost attention! God wants your ear on this! Hear the Word of God! If there is any truth you must get into your heart, it is this ... **you are saved and you will always be saved**!!! You have EVERLASTING LIFE! You possess ETERNAL LIFE! God's Word declares that you *"shall not come into condemnation," "shall never perish,"* and have *"passed from death unto life!!!" (John 5:24).* *[Emphasis added]*

But as earnestly as God desires that you have this knowledge, someone will fight just as earnestly to take it from you! There is a personal devil who is alive and lives for one purpose — to destroy you. He knows that you are saved and that he can no longer harm your soul, but how he longs to ruin your service for God. He trembles in fear that you may speak out about your new-found faith and introduce your friends and family to Christ. He uses an old, time-tested weapon — doubt. He will do all in his power to rob you of your faith and trust in the written Word of God and will attempt to convince you to base your eternal

13

life on your feelings or your experiences.

Recently I had the joy of leading a man to Christ. After he had prayed, I asked him, "Dave, can I talk you out of this?" "No," he said. "Can your friends talk you out of this!" "No." "Well, Dave," I asked, "Can the devil talk you out of it ... because he is certainly going to try!" Scripture bears this out: *"Be sober, be vigilant; because your adversary the devil, as a roaring lion, walketh about, seeking whom he may devour." (I Peter 5:8).*

Why does Satan work so feverishly to destroy the believer? What is the sense of urgency that drives him on to devour Christians? Satan understands what many new Christians do not understand. He knows how vitally important a firm assurance is to your future in your new-found faith.

Result of Peace: Satisfaction

The most important thing at this stage of your Christian life is to have complete and total assurance that nothing can ever rob you of your eternal life in Christ Jesus! Why is this so? First of all, because it will rob you of your satisfaction in Christ. Jesus came to earth for some very important reasons, one of which is "... *that they might have life and ... have it more abundantly." (John 10:10).*

It is God's desire that you have a full, rich and satisfying life in His Son, Jesus Christ. Paul tells us that we are *"complete in Him." (Colossians 2:10).* But when a person loses the assurance of that special place in God's love, he no longer sets his *"affections on things above" (Colossians 3:2)* but turns to other things and leaves his "first love." John gives his reasons for writing the epistle of 1 John. *"These things have I written unto you that believe on the name of the Son of God; that ye may know that ye have eternal life, and that ye may believe on the name of the Son of God." (I John 5:13).*

Earlier in this epistle he gives another reason for writing it. *"And these things write we unto you, that your joy may be full." (1 John 1:4).*

Do these statements contradict each other? No, in fact, they complement each other. You see, if you "know that ye have eternal life," you will naturally have full joy! That is God's plan. He inspired John to write an entire epistle just so that you may have full and complete joy in your heart! But God knows that the basis of that joy and satisfaction in your life is your knowledge and assurance of eternal life.

Result of Peace: Service

As a teenager being imminently wiser than my parents, I took it upon myself to leave home and make my own life. I showed how "smart" I was by quitting school and getting a job as a soda jerk in a restaurant. One evening I found myself lying in bed staring at the ceiling. I can remember the thought that went through my head, "Of all the millions of people in this big world, why did God create me?" God heard that question and answered it in ways I never would have imagined. Have you ever wondered if there were some special purpose for your existence? God has a very special purpose for your life. He created you to serve Him. *"For we are his workmanship, created in Christ Jesus **unto good works.**" (Ephesians 2:10). [Emphasis added]*

Think of it! God has a particular and distinct goal for your life. You are not just a number! Not just another cog in the wheel of humanity! You are created for the purpose of "good works." God wants to use you to help others.

God's purpose is to bless others through your good works. Satan's purpose is to rob others of the blessings of your good works. And how does he accomplish this? By robbing you of your assurance. D.L. Moody said, "I have never known a Christian who was any good in the work of Christ who did not have the assurance of his salvation."

During the first part of the construction of the world's largest bridge in San Francisco no safety devices were used, and twenty-three men fell to their deaths. During the construction of the last part of that bridge, a safety net was constructed at the cost of $100,000. It saved lives. At least ten men fell into the net and were saved. But the interesting thing is that the workers got twenty-five percent more work accomplished once they were assured they were safe.

This is true in the Christian's life as well. In fact, King David observed this principle in his own life. After his awful sin of adultery and murder, he lost his joy. He no longer sang of his God. He no longer spoke of the things of God. The fountain of his praise was dried up and his joy had evaporated. After more than a year of this misery, he cried out to God, *"Restore unto me the joy of thy salvation; and uphold me with thy free spirit. Then will I teach transgressors thy ways; and sinners shall be converted unto thee."* (Psalm 51:12-13).

The Christian who has lost his assurance will stop attending church, avoid his Christian friends, stop his witnessing, and lose his song of joy.

I read a fascinating tale of a little country boy who was walking on the side of the road when a man who was lost drove up. The man asked, "Say, fellow, how do you get to town?" The little boy said, "I don't know." "Where does this road go from here?" "I don't know." "What is the name of the street I am on?" "I don't know." "Boy, you sure don't know much, do you?" "I know I ain't lost." And until you know that you ain't lost, you will never enjoy the fruit of your Christian life. Peter knew this when he wrote, *"For if these things be in you, and abound, they make you that ye shall neither be barren nor unfruitful." (2 Peter 1:8).*

Why does one become "barren" and "unfruitful?" Because *"... he that lacketh these things is blind, and cannot see afar off, and hath forgotten that he was purged from his old sins." (2 Peter 1:9).*

There it is! If you lose the assurance of your forgiveness and salvation, the natural result is barrenness and unfruitfulness. We fail to accomplish the good works for which we were created! Our purpose in life is lost! Our goals are disappointed! The lost are not told about their only hope for eternity; the work of God languishes!

Do you see how important it is that you know you are saved? Your stability depends on it, your satisfaction depends on it, and your service depends upon it.

Result of Peace: Separation

Your separation from sin depends upon the assurance of your salvation as well. God's will for your life is that you *"... live soberly, righteously, and godly, in this present world." (Titus 2:12).* You no longer live under the control of the flesh and the devil. You now serve a higher cause, a greater Master. Peter admonishes us to *"... abstain from fleshly lusts which war against the soul." (1 Peter 2:11).*

You walk to a different drumbeat now, you take orders from another drillmaster. Why this change? Because you know that you are saved, you know that you are His and He is yours. Dare you do less than live purely before Him? He loves you and you love Him, and the thought of disappointing Him is intolerable.

On the other hand, if you have lost assurance of your salvation, if you are uncertain of your salvation, you will be tempted to reason differently. You may think ... "if I have lost that relationship with Him, if I am no longer in His family, if I am bound for hell anyway, why bother? Why make the effort? Why speak out against sin? Why fight the devil's plans? If I am doomed and damned, this 'salvation' game never really worked for me after all; and if it didn't work for me, what makes me think it will work for someone else. And if it won't work for them, why bother telling them about it?"

At this point the devil has you right where he wants you. Because you have lost your assurance, you are useless to God, to the lost, and to yourself.

It is at this point that many new Christians give up. Don't let this happen to you, dear friend. You can prevent this awful scenario from living itself out in your life! You can have the victory over such awful consequences!

Chapter Two

"Blasted Assurance"

I had a college friend who could not accept the Bible teaching of eternal salvation, or "eternal security" as it is better known. He felt that one could lose his salvation under certain circumstances. This caused him much grief because he was never certain at any given time whether he was saved or not. It also caused him no end of consternation from the ribbing he received from his friends who unmercifully poked fun at his beliefs.

On one occasion he was invited to speak at a student gathering on Sunday afternoon. Over 500 students were in the student chapel and Mike was introduced. The emcee announced the names of the hymns to be sung in Mike's honor.

"Let's all stand," he boomed out, "and sing two of Mike's favorite hymns: *Ye Must Be Born Again and Again and Again* and *Blasted Assurance.*"

Great laughter erupted as everyone realized the joke was at Mike's expense. But the underlying truth here is no joking matter. Many new believers fail in their Christian walk because they have never acquired a firm assurance about their salvation. Theirs is not a blessed assurance but a "blasted assurance."

How does the Christian lose his assurance? Why does he lose his peace? Why does he doubt his salvation? There are several reasons that this happens.

FEELINGS

I knocked on an apartment door in North Attleboro, Massachusetts. I heard a thudding sound and suddenly the door was flung wide open! I was confronted by a huffing, puffing apparition of womanhood with disheveled hair and arms covered with white foam. In my shock, I couldn't decide whether to laugh or to run. "Come in," she blurted. "The baby is in the sink!" Whereupon she charged madly out of my sight. I cautiously stepped into the apartment.

"I'm in here!" The voice came from my left. I made my way to the kitchen where I saw her. She was not a monster after all. She was just an ordinary mother giving her baby girl a sudsy bath in the kitchen sink.

After getting acquainted, I shared with her the good news of Jesus Christ. Sally was an intelligent pre-law student who analyzed my every word and carefully considered the claims of Christ on her life. After a few insightful questions, she bowed her head with me for prayer. She prayed sincerely and asked Christ to save her. When she finished her prayer, she remained still for a moment, then she slowly lifted her face to mine with a look of constrained anger and disappointment. "I don't feel a thing," she said with an accusing tone.

Somehow, I felt guilty … like I had misled her or had shortchanged her. I searched my mind for some memory of presenting a false hope, but I could find none.

"I thought you were supposed to feel something," she blurted.

"Sally," I said, "you have just met the Lord Jesus for the first time. He is a new friend. When you first meet a new friend, you don't always feel close to him at once. But as you spend time with Him and grow to know Him, you will grow to love Him. Give it time and the feelings will come." That seemed to satisfy her, so after confirming her decision with some Scriptures, I bid her farewell.

Early the next morning I was awakened by the shrill jangling of the phone at my bedside. I groped in the darkness for the source of this annoyance. As I put it to my ear, I heard it ... a high-pitched shriek drilling through my semiconscious state into the marrow of my mind: "I feel it! I feel it!" It was Sally. She had spent much of the night in the Word of God, and the full realization of what had happened had hit her. She just had to call and share the good news with me. Sally is still faithfully serving the Lord and enjoying the blessings of her salvation.

Sally's initial mistake is the same one committed by many new believers. They equate faith with feelings ... salvation with their senses ... hope with happiness. This is a dangerous position to take.

For feelings come and feelings go,
And feelings are deceiving.
My faith is in the Word of God,
Naught else is worth believing.

Martin Luther

The "Presumer"

"The great Dr. Harry Ironside approached a man about his salvation. 'Are you certain that you are saved?' he asked. 'I was converted by Billy Sunday himself!' came the reply. Dr. Ironside wisely observed, 'Mr. Sunday would have been the last of men to put himself in the place of Christ.' Further conversation seemed to elicit the evidence that the person in question had been carried away by admiration for the earnest evangelist and mistook the 'thrill of a handshake' for the Spirit's witness. At least there seemed no real understanding of God's plan of salvation which Billy Sunday preached in such tremendous power. It is well to remember that some vivid emotional experience is not a safe ground of assurance. It is the blood of Christ that makes us safe and the Word of God that makes us sure."[1]

This so-called salvation decision was based on a faulty foundation of feelings. This man was not genuinely saved. He had been deceived to rely on his feelings. He may have been sincere, but he was never saved. He only presumed he was. That is one extreme.

The "Feeler"

The other extreme is the "feeler" ... the person who is genuinely saved and experiences the deepest of emotions. These people stand and testify of their "Damascus Road" (Paul's conversion experience on the road to Damascus as described in Acts chapter nine) experience. They tell of the light, the voice, and the deep feelings they encountered at the time of conversion. They thrill to this obvious confirmation to the certainty of their salvation. They are carried on a wave of emotion for a few days, still basking in the warmth of that blessed experience. But, they have not been grounded in the truths of the Word of God. They have not been warned that the day would come when the feelings flee like the morning vapor under the sun. When the feelings wane and weaken, they become worried, then frightened. Because they have equated their salvation with their feelings, they fear that since the feelings are gone so is the salvation. They become disillusioned. They cry out to God to bring back the blessing. They seek another emotional experience to confirm the first one.

Oh, how my heart goes out to this person! He will soon drift away from the Lord if he does not understand the Bible teaching on this subject.

The "Rubber Stamp"

Then there is the person who listens in awe at the testimony of the "feeler" described above. He concludes that when he finally goes to the altar to receive Christ, he will share a similar experience. Finally that day arrives. He listens to the preaching … he makes his way to the altar where he prays to trust Christ into as his Savior. He waits. Nothing happens. He gets off his knees. "No feeling, no salvation," he concludes. "It just wasn't meant to be," he sadly admits.

One man presumes he is saved and isn't, the other is saved but bases it on his feelings, and the third is saved but concludes he is not because he didn't feel anything. How dangerous and misleading these feelings can be.

Don't misunderstand me. It is not wrong to feel something when you get saved. But it is wrong to seek these feelings or to depend upon them as evidence of true salvation.

Some people are saved and they laugh, some cry, some do nothing. Your emotional reaction is more a reflection of your individual make-up and temperament than the genuineness of your salvation.

I have conducted dozens of marriages during my years as a pastor. It is interesting to observe the different reactions on the part of the bride and groom. I have seen some get the "giggles" as they stand at the altar, while others weep uncontrollably. Still others shake like a leaf in a thunderstorm while some are stone rigid and ghostly white. None of these reactions strengthen or weaken the validity of their nuptial. One is just as married as the other.

At my wedding reception I was asked by a friend, "Well Binney, how does it feel to be married?" I honestly didn't know at that time. I was still numb with joy. My computer was short-circuited. Did that mean that I wasn't married? Absolutely not. How did I know? Because I held in my hand a piece of paper signed by the pastor and a couple of witnesses that declared, in no uncertain terms, that James Dale Binney and Sandra Lee Canavan had been united in holy matrimony. I didn't have to rely on my feelings. I had it in writing!

Likewise I do not have to rely upon my feelings to know that I am saved. I have it in writing!!! *"These things have I <u>written</u> unto you that believe on the name of the Son of God; that ye may KNOW* (not think, wish, hope or feel) *that ye have eternal life." (1 John 5:13).* [Emphasis added]

The "Gospel Train"

Let me tell you about the Gospel Train. It is a unique vehicle which guarantees that you will get to Heaven. It has only

three cars, but each of them is a very important part of the whole.
The engine is called "FACT" and can run all by itself. It doesn't
need the help of any other cars to move forward. The passenger
car is labeled "FAITH" and is attached to the engine. The
caboose of this unusual train is termed "FEELINGS." Our train
looks something like this:

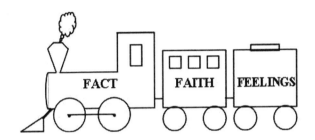

Now the engine can run all by itself. It doesn't need the
help of faith or feelings. The Word of God is FACT. It says. "...
Believe on the Lord Jesus Christ, and thou shalt be saved." (Acts
16:31). That is an honest-to-goodness fact. Whether a person
has faith in it or not, the fact remains. It stands alone. Like the
engine, it runs on its own energy. It can move ahead with or
without the other cars.

The FAITH car, on the other hand, is dependent upon
FACT. Once it is attached, it becomes a part of the train, but it
cannot propel itself alone. When you put your FAITH in the
FACT of God's promise, you were saved. The train of salvation
is now functional, but it is not complete. It lacks a caboose. The
caboose houses some men who are called out in times of trouble to
repair the train and keep it running. The caboose is FEELINGS.
Feelings are a very real part of the salvation train. *"... the joy of
the Lord is your strength."* (Nehemiah 8:10). Nehemiah said this

25

and for very good reason. God never intended for us to endure a dry, tasteless brand of Christianity. He desires for us to have joy, peace, love, and the other ingredients of the abundant life.

If we never experience the joy of the Lord, it may be that we have never been saved. But FEELINGS are attached to FAITH and dependent upon it. The caboose does not pull the train; it follows it. The caboose is not always attached, but the train will still travel.

If you can get this concept clear in your mind, it will save you much heartache in the future. See the FACT. Put your FAITH in the FACT, and the FEELINGS will follow in God's time and in God's way.

If we make the pursuit of feelings our aim in life, we will always be disappointed because feelings are out of our realm of control. But we can always give ourselves to the fact of God's Holy Word, and we can control the growth of faith.

"Greased Pig" Christianity

"Faith cometh by ... the Word of God." (Romans 10:17). When I think of someone chasing after elusive feelings, I am reminded of a greased-pig chase I attended. The hapless pig was covered from head to toe with a thick coat of lard (oh, the indignity of it ...) and released into an arena of tense and determined young people. With the cry of the kids and the squeal of the pig, the race was on! One after another, the determined chasers lay their hands upon the body or appendages of the frantic porker. Time and time again he slipped from their clutches.

26

So it is with feelings … we chase them and hunt them down, only to find that they slip out of our eager grasp. This is "greased pig" Christianity. Dr. Bob Jones, Sr. often used to say, "Happiness is stumbled upon in the pathway of duty." In other words, feelings are the dividends that God pays on the investment of obedience.

Peter had fished all night and caught nothing. Jesus climbed into the boat with him and told him how to fish. Peter obeyed and the boat was filled to overflowing with slippery, writhing fish. (Luke 5). This is what Peter had worked all night for. But what does Peter do now? He falls down on his knees at the feet of Jesus and has eyes only for Him. What had happened to Peter? He had learned to love the Blesser more than the blessings, to obey God's Word rather than follow his feelings. Dedicate yourself to following the Blesser and the blessing will be yours. Obey His Word and the feelings will follow. Dr. Ironside relates this story in his inspiring book, *Full Assurance.*

> Many years ago I was holding a series of evangelistic meetings in a little country schoolhouse some miles out of Santa Cruz, California. One day I was out driving with a kindly old gentleman who was attending the services nightly but who was far from being sure of his personal salvation. As we drove along a beautiful winding road, I put the definite question to him. "Have you peace with God?" He drew rein at once, stopped the horse and exclaimed, "Now that's what I brought you here for. I won't go another foot until I know I am saved ."

"How do you expect to find out?" I inquired.

"Well, that is what puzzles me. I want a definite witness, something that I cannot be mistaken about."

"Just what would you consider definite, some inward emotional stirring!"

"I can hardly say, only most folks tell us they felt some powerful change when they got religion. I have been seeking that for years, but it has always eluded me."

"Getting religion is one thing; trusting Christ may be quite another. But now suppose you were seeking salvation, and suddenly there came to you a very happy feeling, would you be sure then that you were saved?"

"Well, I think I would."

"Then, suppose you went through life resting on that experience, and at last came down to the hour of death. Imagine Satan telling you that you were lost and would soon be beyond hope of mercy, what would you say to him? Would you tell him that you knew all was well because you had such a happy emotional experience years before? What if he should declare that it was he who gave you that happy feeling in order to deceive you; could you prove it was not?"

"No," he answered thoughtfully, "I couldn't. I see that a happy feeling is not enough."

"What would be enough?"

"If I could get some definite word in a vision or a message from an angel, then I could be sure."

"But suppose you had a vision of a glorious angel and he told you your sins were forgiven, would that really be enough to rest on?"

"I think it would. One ought to be certain if an angel said it was all right."

"But if you were dying and Satan was there to disturb you and told you that you were lost after all, what could you say?"

"Why, I'd tell him an angel told me I was saved."

"But if he said, 'I was that angel, transformed myself into an angel of light to deceive you. And now you are where I wanted you – you will be lost forever.' What then could you say?"

He pondered a moment or two and then replied, "I see you are right; the word of an angel won't do."

"But now," I said, "God has given

something better than happy feelings, something more dependable than the voice of an angel. He has given His Son to die for your sins, and He has testified in His own unalterable Word that if you trust Him, all your sins are gone. Listen to this: 'To him give all the prophets witness, that through his name whosoever believeth in him shall receive remission of sins.' These are the words of God spoken through His apostle Peter as recorded in Acts 10:43.

"Then here in 1 John 5:13 which says, 'These things have I written unto you that believe on the name of the Son of God; that ye may know that ye have eternal life.' Are these words addressed to you? Do you believe on the Name of the Son of God?"

"I do, sir, I do indeed! I know He is the Son of God, and I know He died for me."

"Then see what He tells you, 'Ye may know that ye have eternal life.' Is not this enough to rest upon? It is a letter from heaven directed expressly to you. How can you refuse to accept what God has told you? Can you not believe Him? Is He not more to be depended on than an angel or than aroused emotions? Can you not take Him at His word and rest upon it for the forgiveness of your sins?

"Now suppose that as you are dying Satan

comes to you and insists that you are lost but you reply, 'No, Satan, you cannot terrify me now. I rest on the Word of the living God, and He tells me I have eternal life and also the remission of all my sins.' Can you not do this now? Will you not bow your head and tell God you will be saved on His terms by coming to Him as a repentant sinner and trusting His Word concerning His blessed Son?"

The old man dropped his eyes and I saw that he was deeply stirred. His lips were moving in prayer. Suddenly he looked up and touching the horse lightly with his whip exclaimed, "Giddap! It's all clear now. This is what I've wanted for years."

"That night at the meeting he came to the front and told the audience that what he had sought in vain for half a lifetime he had found when he believed the message of God's Word about what Jesus had done to save sinners. For several years he was a regular correspondent of mine until the Lord took him home – a joyous saint whose doubts and fears had all been banished when he rested on the sure Word of God. His was the full assurance of faith."

"And please don't misunderstand me. I do not discount the emotional element in conversion, but I insist it will not do to rely upon it as an evidence that one has been forgiven. When a man is awakened by the Spirit of God to realize something of his lost, undone condition, it would be strange indeed if his emotions were not aroused. When he is brought to repentance, that is, to a complete change of attitude toward his sins, toward himself and toward God, we need not be surprised to see the tears of penitence coursing down his cheeks. And when he rests his soul on what God has said and receives in faith the Spirit's witness, *"Their sins and iniquities will I remember no more,"* it would be unthinkable but that, like Wesley, his heart should be strangely warmed as he rejoiced in God's salvation.

"What I am trying to make plain is that assurance isn't based upon any emotional change; but whatever emotional experience there may be, it will be the result of accepting the testimony of the Lord given in the Scriptures. Faith rests on the naked Word of God. That Word believed gives full assurance. Then the Holy Spirit comes to dwell in the believer's heart and to conform him to Christ. Growth in grace follows naturally when the soul has trusted Christ and entered into peace with God."[2]

One of the greatest dangers facing the new believer is the misleading feelings that they tend to rely upon. But there is another hidden pitfall in the Christian life.

FAILURE

A pastor relates this story. At the conclusion of a mass meeting, I was greeting people when a distinguished-looking man approached me and asked, "May I talk with you about my salvation? I'm desperately confused." He went on to state that he had acknowledged the Lord as Savior but had little peace and Christian confidence. "As I listened to your message I decided I must settle it."

I replied, "First, look into your life to discover if all is right between yourself and the Lord. Carnal believers are usually full of doubts. If the Holy Spirit is grieved through self-will or sin, He cannot witness effectively to your salvation because there is contradiction. For this reason the witness of the Holy Spirit is often dimmed. Second, after discovering the wrong, openly confess it to the Lord. Third, deal with it and do works to prove your repentance."

"That's it," he interrupted. "I've grown careless; there's sin in my life, and I must make it right."

We bowed our heads in a holy hush as he sought God's gracious forgiveness. It was evident that the Lord was in the room, for when we arose from our knees the doctor was changed. His expression, his voice, his whole attitude radiated blessed assurance. Careless living will always create doubt, but the opposite is also true. Doubt leads to careless living.[3]

Don't make the mistake of assuming that because you are saved your sinning days are behind you. This is a deadly philosophy and one that Satan exploits to full advantage with new Christians.

If you believe that "as a Christian I cannot sin" or "I will not sin because I am a Christian," you will experience bitter disappointment when you do sin. I have seen Christians so devastated by the fact of their failure that they never recovered from their disappointment. You *will* sin, dear friend.

I don't say that to discourage you but to encourage you. I want you to avoid that awful snare of unrealistic expectations about your walk with God.

"If we say that we have no sin, we deceive ourselves, and the truth is not in us. If we say that we have not sinned, we make him [God] *a liar, and his word is not in us." (1 John 1:8, 10).* The Apostle John penned these words to new converts in the faith whom he affectionately referred to as "little children." He wanted these new Christians to know that they would sin. He wanted to prepare them for the inevitable.

When I came to the Lord as a 17-year-old boy, the man who led me to Christ recommended that I get alone and read the book of 1 John. I marveled as I read the passage from which I quoted above. I am glad that I learned this important principle because later, when I did fail my Lord, I was able to overcome the temptation of giving in to the disappointment. Why? Because in this same passage there is a solution to the problem as well. *"If we confess our sins, he is faithful and just to forgive us our sins, and to cleanse us from all unrighteousness." (1 John 1:9).* John wisely included the statement of victory along with the statement of failure.

I recall kneeling in the prayer room at Bible school and pouring out my broken heart to Jesus. I confessed my sin, my failure, my disobedience, and what sweet peace flooded my soul! I knew I was forgiven ... the Bible said so! I was cleansed ... the Bible said so. Everything was alright with my Heavenly Father. The Bible says so!

When I stood at the bar of judgment and heard the accusations made against me, I had a lawyer right beside me to speak out in my defense. *"If any man sin, we have an advocate* [defense attorney] *with the Father, Jesus Christ the righteous" (1 John 2:1).* He reminds the Judge that *"the blood of Jesus Christ his Son cleanseth us from all sin." (1 John 1:7).*

It was a great day when I realized that the Father listens to my lawyer, Jesus Christ. And what a thrill it was when I realized that He was not merely speaking to the Father, but He was speaking to me as well!

Don't let the devil bully you into believing that you are washed up because you have failed as a Christian. When you sin, confess it, and believe God by faith to cleanse your heart and life!

FELLOWSHIP VS. RELATIONSHIP

I have talked with many travelers on the road of the Christian walk, and I have found a common barrier to their victory. They confuse "fellowship" with God and a "relationship" with God. There is an important distinction between these two words.

My son Jonathan was a typical energetic toddler who demanded our full-time attention. On one occasion we failed in this attention and suffered the consequences.

My wife I were in the kitchen preparing for a meal when we heard a dull thudding sound from the front room, followed by the sound of running water. Upon investigating, we discovered Jonathan with a hammer tightly clenched in his little fist and a look of rapturous delight upon his face. Beside him stood our 10-gallon aquarium with a sizeable hole in its side. At Jonathan's water-soaked feet were the former contents of the tank. The water was still gurgling through the fibers of the carpet, and the fish tossed and gasped in frantic desperation on the floor With a look of innocent pride Jonathan boldly proclaimed, "Daddy, I let dem fishies out!" I reminded myself of divine parental responsibilities, I counted to ten, I tried to conjure up remembrances of applicable Bible verses for the occasion, but I could tell by the gradually sinking countenance of my son that I was failing woefully. To summarize the situation, I will simply say that our fellowship was broken. I sent Jonathan to his room and I treated the problem. Jonathan was still my son ... I was still his father. That vital relationship was not changed. But our fellowship certainly was.

God is our Heavenly Father. That wonderful relationship will never change! The Lord Jesus taught His disciples to envision Him as *"Our father which art in Heaven ..." (Matthew 6:9)*. He is called the *"everlasting Father" (Isaiah 9:6)* and the *"Father ... with whom is no variableness, neither shadow of turning." (James 1:17)*. Our Heavenly Father makes a wonderful promise: *"I will never leave thee nor forsake thee." (Hebrews 13:5)*. Ours is an *eternal* relationship! Our relationship with Him will *never* change!

On one occasion, Jonathan came home crestfallen, "I don't have any friends," he sadly bemoaned. I could see that this was a deep wound in his spirit so I took him aside and looked intently into his troubled face. "Son," I said, "there is one thing I want you never, ever to forget. No matter what happens in your life, I want you to know that you will always have a home with your Mom and me where there will always be love for you." He stared back into my eyes, in deep thought for a moment. "Thanks, Dad!" he said and gave me a big bear hug. God is like that. He promises always to be there and never to leave us. Our relationship with God as our Father can never change! What security there is in such great and precious promises!

On the other hand, our fellowship with God can change, and it can change quickly. My toddler son realized that he had done wrong in letting the "fishies" out, and the result was that our closeness was severed. Our fellowship was broken. That brokenness was not restored until he realized his sin and confessed it. That is God's way of dealing with the sin of His children. *"For whom the Lord loveth he chasteneth, and scourgeth every son whom he receiveth ... God dealeth with you as with sons; for what son is he whom the father chasteneth not?" (Hebrews 12:6-7).*

What is it that breaks our fellowship with our heavenly Father? It is sin. And only sin has the power to accomplish this! But as powerful as sin is, God's grace is even more powerful. *"... where sin abounded, grace did much more abound." (Romans 5:20).*

Broken fellowship with God can be dealt with instantly. There is no need to endure the agony of a distanced God when we can bask in the warmth of His fellowship continually. Make it a practice that the instant you realize you have sinned you bow your head and confess your sin to your Father. Immediately, instantly, on the spot, He will forgive you and restore you to full fellowship with Him.

Don't confuse a fractured, broken fellowship with a ruined relationship. Nothing can rob you of your eternal life! If that could happen, it would not be eternal but temporary. Understand that the distance you sense between you and God is a severed fellowship, and it can be restored whenever you confess it as sin.

(**Note:** To further your understanding about true confession, take time now to read the article in the Appendix entitled "Cleaning Out the Cow Stall.")

FRIENDSHIPS

Unsaved Friends

We have seen that a misunderstanding about feelings, failure and fellowship are serious barriers in our growth in the Christian life. Another one is the wrong kind of friends.

The Bible clearly condemns our friendship with certain types of people. The first of these is the unsaved person. *"Be ye not unequally yoked together with unbelievers ..." (2 Corinthians 6:14). "Blessed is the man that walketh not in the counsel of the ungodly ..." (Psalm 1:1). "Enter not into the path of the wicked, and go not in the way of evil men." (Proverbs 4:14). "Be not thou envious against evil men, neither desire to be with them." (Proverbs 24:1).*

We are not to yoke up with the unbeliever, walk in their counsel, enter into their path, nor desire to be with them. As you read these words, you may see the faces of your friends in your mind's eye. You may wonder why the Bible makes such harsh requirements. After all, these have been your friends for years. My heart goes out to you because those are the precise feelings I had many years ago when I first came to Christ. Don't stop reading!!! God has more to say to you about this. I want to help you to understand the reasons for this commandment.

Carnal Friends

Another type of relationship that God condemns is that between the godly Christian and the Christian who is not living right. *"But now I have written unto you not to keep company, if any man that is called a brother be a fornicator, or covetous, or an idolater, or a railer, or a drunkard, or an extortioner; with such an one no not to eat." (1 Corinthians 5:11). "Now I beseech you, brethren, mark them which cause divisions ... and avoid them." (Romans 16:17). "...there are some which walk among you disorderly, working not at all ... withdraw yourselves from every brother that walketh disorderly." (2 Thessalonians 3:11, 6).*

Paul warns us about the man who is *"destitute of the truth supposing that gain is godliness: from such withdraw thyself." (1 Timothy 6:5).*

It saddens me to say it, but there are some people in the churches of America who fit the descriptions in the above verses. God lovingly warns His children to stay away from them. These include fornicators (sexually sinful), covetous (those who lust after material things of others), idolaters (those who put something or someone else before God). railers (those who speaks against another with the intention of harming their reputation), drunkards, and extortioners (those who take advantage of another for financial gain). Also included are those who cause divisions, the lazy who will not work, and those who believe that material prosperity is equal to godliness.

God's command regarding associating with these people is clear: put them *"away,"* *"avoid them,"* *"withdraw yourselves from them,"* *"with such a one no not to eat."* Furthermore, the Scriptures plainly declare: *"Make no friendship with an angry man; and with a furious man thou shalt not go: Lest thou learn his ways, and get a snare to thy soul."* *(Proverbs 22:24-25).*

The saintly Matthew Henry gives some keen insight into this passage: "Here is a good caution against being intimate with a passionate man. It is the law of friendship that we accommodate ourselves to our friends and be ready to serve them; and, therefore, we ought to be wise and wary in the choice of a friend that we come not under that sacred tie to any one whom it would be our folly to accommodate ourselves to. Though we must be civil to all, yet we must be careful whom we lay in our bosoms and contracts a familiarity with. And, among others, a man who is easily provoked, touchy and apt to resent affronts, who, when he is in a passion, cares not what he says or does, but grows outrageous, such a one is not fit to be made a friend or companion, for he will be ever and anon angry with us and that will be our trouble, and he will expect that we should, like him, be angry with others, and that will be our sin.

"Good cause given for this caution: 'Lest thou learn his way.' Those we go with, we are apt to grow like. It is dangerous conversing with those that throw about the sparks of their passion. We shall thereby get a snare to our souls, for a disposition to anger is a great snare to any man, and an occasion of much sin. He does not say, 'Lest thou have ill language given thee or get a broken head' but, which is much worse. 'Lest thou imitate him, to humor him, and so contract an ill habit.'"[4]

As an unsaved teenager, I had many friends in school. I attended T.C. Howe High School in Indianapolis, Indiana, a school of several thousand students. Each week I went with my friends to a local, liberal church for a teen dance.

After I trusted Christ as my Saviour, I was advised by a mature Christian not to return to those dances again. Well, I certainly couldn't understand that! "Why not?" I asked indignantly! My friend patiently explained: "Jim, suppose I am on the floor and you get up on this chair … (which I did). Now, you try to pull me up there, while I try to pull you down to my level." Obviously, he won that game.

He explained to me that evil affects righteousness in similar situations more quickly than righteousness changes evil. *"Iron sharpeneth iron; so a man sharpeneth the countenance of his friend." (Proverbs 27:17).*

If two pieces of iron are rubbed together, one piece will in time make an impression upon the other. Of course, it is the hard piece that will impress the soft piece. Likewise, in our friendships, it is an unchangeable law that one person will always make an impression upon another.

In our naïve love, we foolishly hope to change our wayward friend by our godly influence. But as Christians, our hearts have been tenderized and softened by the presence of the loving Holy Spirit of God. As a Spirit-softened believer comes into contact with a sin-hardened friend, it is the hardened who makes the greater impression. Ungodliness will pull godliness down; hardness will impress softness.

But I protested to my friend that I would not be so easily

influenced. I determined to keep my friends and my Christianity, too. I went back to the old hangout with a carload of friends. I justified this decision by making my time there one of witnessing for Christ. After all, if I could win my friends to Christ, I could keep them as my friends. Nothing had changed, except me. I felt strangely uncomfortable being there, but I didn't want my old friends to think that I was a "holy Joe" or that I was deserting them.

I began dancing with a girlfriend (Strange that dancing with boys never appealed to me … is there a hidden truth there about the appeal of dancing?) and as we were gyrating to the beat, I said, "Are you saved?" "What did you say?" she blurted! I felt a knot of uneasiness under my breastbone. I repeated, "Are you saved? Are you a Christian?" "Are you?" she demanded. I was feeling more uncomfortable all the time. "Yes," I admitted, some-what weakly. Stopping her dancing, she put her hands on her hips, looked me squarely in the eyes, and said, "THEN WHAT ARE YOU DOING HERE?"

Indeed, what was I doing here? Was I trying to win a sinner or keep a friend? Was I attempting to prove that one could be saved and still be "cool?" I was rebuked by this challenge to my life-style as a believer. This unsaved girl had higher standards for my Christianity than I did. I realized with shame that I had let the Lord down by going to that place and thinking I could make a difference in an unsaved girl's life without living an example before her. I left the dance that night a changed person. I con-fessed my sin to God and decided then and there never again to frequent a dance hall. I resolved that my friends would be

Christians only. I would soon learn the high price of such a conviction.

After I had been saved for a while and was working in a department store, a teenage girl came up to me, accompanied by her little brother, in order to purchase some clothing for him. As I assisted her, we struck up a lively conversation. We chatted for a while and they left. The next day she was back … alone. As she coyly fingered some clothing at a distance, I made my way to her and invited her out to lunch. Things progressed quickly, and after a period of casual dating, she invited me to her home to meet her parents and to have dinner with them. I consented despite a growing uneasiness about her spiritual state. I determined that I was going to talk with her about her salvation.

After we had dinner, we went into the parlor of their house to talk. I knew what I had to do. "Polly," I asked, "are you saved? If you were to die today, are you certain that you would be in heaven?" "That's a strange question," she replied. After giving it some thought, she admitted that she was not sure of eternal life. I went through the plan of salvation carefully with her and asked her if she would be willing to trust Christ as her personal Saviour. "Not right now … maybe later," she answered.

I took a deep breath. "Polly," I said, "I'm afraid that I can no longer date you." With astonishment in her eyes she demanded, "Why not?" I showed her a verse in my New Testament. *"Be ye not unequally yoked together with unbelievers: for what fellowship hath righteousness with unrighteousness? and what communion hath light with darkness?" (2 Corinthians 6:14)*

"Polly," I said, "God's commandment is that the saved should not fellowship with the unsaved. I must obey God. I like you very much, and I would like to continue dating you, but I cannot do that and obey God. I am very sorry. This hurts me very much, and I know it must hurt you, too, but I must make this decision. If you ever decide to be saved, call me to let me know and we will get together again." With that I left brokenhearted, expecting never to hear from her again.

A couple of months later I got a phone call on the dorm floor. "Jim" the voice said excitedly, "this is Polly! Guess what?! I was at an evangelistic meeting last night, and after the sermon, I went forward to pray! I got saved! I asked Jesus to come into my heart! I couldn't forget what you had told me. I knew that I would never see you again if I did not become a Christian, but more than that, I realized how empty my life was without Christ. Now I know that if I died I would be in Heaven! Isn't it neat?!"

It was very neat! What our friendship could not accomplish, our separation did! God knew exactly what He was doing when He commanded that I not attempt to fellowship with an unsaved girl. He knew she would not come to Christ unless something big enough jarred her into an awareness of her lost condition.

God's Purpose For Separation From Friends

God is not unfair when He tells you to separate from your friends. He has a purpose in it. What is that purpose? First of all, He wants to remove you from a harmful influence upon your life, *"Lest thou learn his ways, and get a snare to thy soul,"*

(*Proverbs 22:25*), "*... a man sharpeneth the countenance of his friend.*" (*Proverbs 27:17*).

These verses tell us that another's life can become a snare to our own, that their influence can shape and mold our very countenance. God loves us and desires to protect us from such damaging relationships.

Secondly, He knows that there can exist no true fellowship between you and the wicked. "*For what fellowship hath righteousness with unrighteousness? and what communion hath light with darkness? And what concord hath Christ with Belial? or what part hath he that believeth with an infidel? And what agreement hath the temple of God with idols? for ye are the temple of the living God.*" (*2 Corinthians 6:14-16*).

Whatever else your relationship with the ungodly produces, it is not true love. Why do I say this? Because, unless a person is close to God, he cannot experience true love. "*... love is of God; and every one that loveth is born of God, and knoweth God. He that loveth not knoweth not God; for God is love.*" (*1 John 4:7-8*).

John is saying that true love originates with God , Who is love and the source of all love. If a person doesn't know God, he cannot love with spiritual love. Spiritual love is the goal of every relationship. We are commanded to "*love one another*" (*1 John 4:11*). The love mentioned here is spiritual love.

There is no doubt that deep emotional feelings and even physical intimacy can exist, but God wants you to experience the best love you possibly can. He is the only source of this love, and it cannot be found anywhere apart from Him. Oh, believe me, there are plenty of lesser forms of this love which we confuse with the real thing. The devaluation of this true love is evident in such statements as "I love pizza" or "I love football."

Another reason we should avoid unspiritual friendships is because it is the command of God. There have been times in my life that I have failed to understand the reason for some of God's requirements upon my life. But I have learned that God is all wise, and He knows what I do not know. I know that God loves me; and when you combine the wisdom of God with the love of God, I realize that He wants only the best for me. It boils down to this ... I must trust Him. I saw a plaque on a wall that said, "God said it; I believe it; that settles it!" But to be precise, it should read: "God said it; that settles it whether I believe it or not." To obey God's command is to find a blessing. To disobey is to lose God's blessings. *"Wherefore come out from among them, and be ye separate, saith the Lord, and touch not the unclean thing; and* [Here's the blessing] *I will receive you, And will be a Father unto you, and ye shall be my sons and daughters, saith the Lord Almighty."* *(2 Corinthians 6:17-18).*

God wants to bless you, therefore He provides a way to achieve His goal. That way is the way of obedience. In this passage of scripture, the command is to separate yourself from unsaved friends. The result ... the favor and blessings of God!

As important as it is that we understand the negative impact of ungodly influence, the lack of true fellowship, the importance of obedience, and the blessings of God, there is another dimension that demands our consideration. All of these affect us personally and are the cause of blessings upon our lives. But as much as God wants to bless us, He wants to reach the unsaved and the ungodly as well. He desires that they receive the blessings described above as much as He wants us to receive them.

But here we encounter a real problem; the Christian can actually be a hindrance to the lost person in need of a Savior. Let me explain. He joins the church, gives his money, lends his talent and time to charitable projects, etc. Outwardly he appears very religious, but inwardly he is full of sin. Jesus likens them unto *"whited sepulchres,* [tombs painted white] *which indeed appear beautiful outward, but are within full of dead men's bones, and of all uncleanness." (Matthew 23:27).*

One of sinful man's favorite ways of justifying his sinful lifestyle is to gain the favor of the religious and the spiritual. He seeks out opportunities to identify himself with these people. He may join the church, teach a Sunday school class, sing in the choir, and serve on the board. He may choose his friends from among the Christians he knows. He enrolls his children in a Christian school to perpetuate his religiosity and to hide his sin. He is comfortable with his hypocrisy and his pseudo-spirituality and it is the proximity of his Christian friends that give him this false sense of security. This is not to say that everyone who does these things is sinful — not by any means. But many in the ranks of the outwardly religious are, in fact, unsaved.

When the true believers remove themselves from him, however, he is shocked into self-examination, a process that is desperately needed to bring him to true repentance. This is the ultimate reason for God's command to withdraw yourself from them. When I withdrew myself from Polly, she realized, for the first time in her life, that she was lost and needed a Saviour. If I had continued the relationship, that may never have happened.

The result of the first four reasons discussed above is self-satisfaction and blessing. The greater result of this reason for separation from the ungodly goes beyond self benefit and extends to the very salvation of the lost.

Therefore, we must separate from the unsaved and the ungodly Christians to activate within them a sense of godly sorrow and conviction unto repentance. In 1 Corinthians chapter 5, the Apostle Paul writes of a horrible sin present in the church of Corinth. One of the men was immoral with a woman. But this woman was his stepmother! *"It is reported commonly that there is fornication among you, and such fornication as is not so much as named among the Gentiles, that one should have his father's wife."* *(1 Corinthians 5:1).*

This man was in the circle of those who are "of God." Somebody might say, "The way to help him is to keep him in the circle, let him sit down with you at the communion table, do not be hard on him, try to win him back, throw your arms of love about him and sympathize with him." But the unrepentant man will be more hardened in his iniquity if you do that. Put him outside in the devil's domain, let him know that he has forfeited all title to a place with the people of God – that he had been put back into the world where Satan rules. That is what Paul means when he says, *"... deliver such an one unto Satan for the destruction of the flesh ..."(1 Corinthians 5:5).*

What has caused all this trouble? The activity of the flesh. Very well, put him out in that sphere where he will find out that it is an "... *evil and bitter*" thing to forsake the "*Lord his God.*" *(Jeremiah 2:19).* When he finds himself abhorred by men and women who love Christ, when he finds his sin is a stench in the nostrils of Christian people, he may break before God. If, in spite of his sin, he has really been born again, he will break. If he has been a false professor, he will plunge deeper and deeper into evil things. *"Deliver such an one unto Satan for the destruction of the flesh, that the spirit may be saved in the day of the Lord Jesus."* (1 Corinthians 5:5). We do not like to carry out extreme commands like these, but this is the Word of God. The greatest kindness that the people of God can do to a man who is deliberately going on in willful sin is to refuse Christian fellowship to him. As long as you treat him as a brother, he will only be puffed up in his ungodly way, and it will be harder to reach him. But if you obey the Word, God will work toward his recovery and restoration."[5]

One of the most common reasons for new converts to fall away from their new-found faith is because of the influence of their unspiritual friends. It may be necessary for you to choose Christ over a friend. Thousands of believers before you have made the same decision. But God will not leave you friendless. *"... there is a friend that sticketh closer than a brother."* *(Proverbs 18:24).* That friend is Jesus. And what a friend He is!

> What a Friend we have in Jesus,
> All our sins and griefs to bear!
>
> What a privilege to carry
> Ev'rything to God in prayer!
>
> Can we find a friend so faithful
> Who will all our sorrows share?
> Joseph Scriven, 1819-1886

> There is not another friend like the Lord Jesus Christ.
>
> There's not a friend like the lowly Jesus—
> No, not one! No, not one!
>
> Johnson Oatman, Jr., 1895

But God gives you other friends besides Jesus. He surrounds you with other children of God. These are your brothers and sisters in the family of God. God has provided these friends to love you, to pray for you, to encourage you and to support you. Look around your circle of new Christian friends. Choose the most spiritual, the one who really seems to love the Lord. Befriend that person whom you might find to be an encouragement in your new walk with Christ.

As you continue your new life, you are learning that the barriers and pitfalls surrounding of assurance are many. There is yet another one that you might face in your life as a Christian, and that is the pitfall of forgetfulness.

FORGETFULNESS

By this I mean that it is possible to forget that you have been saved. *"But he that lacketh these things is blind, and cannot see afar off, and hath forgotten that he was purged from his old sins." (2 Peter 1:9).*

The Apostle Peter is telling us that it is possible for the believer to come to a place in his life that, although he has been genuinely saved, he can forget that blessed event and lose all assurance of his salvation. How does one avoid this? Pause here to read carefully the entire first chapter of 2 Peter and you will see the answer.

Peter speaks of the marvelous results of becoming a child of God. He describes it as being *"... partaker of the divine nature" (2 Peter 1:4)*, but he immediately adds that there is more required as a believer.

*"And beside this, **giving all diligence** ..." (2 Peter 1:5)* *[Emphasis added]*. Incorporated into this simple statement is one of the most important principles the recent convert can learn! The word "diligence" means "to exert oneself," "to endeavor."[6] This involves "intense effort" and carries with it the meaning of a continual process rather than a one-time effort. In other words, the assurance that God desires for you is the result of persistent effort and untiring diligence.

It is a matter of research that forty days of intense effort are required to rehabituate a pattern of thinking. In other words, until the Christian walk becomes as automatic and habitual as your former life, it will demand special effort to change from your former thoughts and actions. From the time of your decision for Christ until the time of thinking and acting differently, at least forty days of real effort will be required. That is not to say that **only** forty days are required – that may be a bare minimum – but **at least** forty days are required. In truth, this process of *"renewing of your mind" (Romans 12:2)* and putting *"off the old,"* and putting *"on the new" (Colossians 3:9-10)* will require the rest of your natural life. But during the crucial first days of your new life in Christ, it is especially important to make every effort to establish yourself in the faith.

When a person first comes to Christ, there is an initial phenomenon of spontaneous momentum that propels him forward in the new-found excitement of his faith. Many young converts, like a novice surfer who misjudges the distance to the beach, make the mistake of riding that wave of effortless euphoria without realizing that it will eventually crash upon the shore.

How many well-intentioned but misinformed Christians awake to find themselves beached before they realize it? Beware at this point, dear friend. Your Christian walk is a relationship with the Lord Jesus Christ, and, like any relationship, it requires effort to sustain it and diligence to enlarge it. For example, the scriptures admonish us to be diligent in purity. *"... be diligent that ye may be found of him in peace, without spot, and blameless." (2 Peter 3:14).*

We need to be diligent to rule our hearts. *"Keep thy heart with all diligence; for out of it are the issues of life." (Proverbs 4:23).*

We must apply diligence in studying the Bible. *"Study to shew thyself approved unto God, a workman that needeth not to be ashamed ..." (2 Timothy 2:15).*

There will be times when you will be discouraged in your Christian life. It will seem that you are not making progress at all or, even worse, that you seem to be regressing. Paul knew this when he wrote, *"And let us not be weary in well-doing: for in due season we shall reap, if we faint not." (Galatians 6:9).* Continual effort and persistent diligence is necessary for victory.

If you are still riding that exciting wave of emotion which accompanied your salvation, understand that you must begin now to be diligent. If you have already been beached and are wondering why the wave has stopped, don't be alarmed. Start now to apply diligence that is required to be sure of your salvation. Determine now, before you go any further, that you will commit yourself to make every effort required to make your life count for God! Ask God to empower you to continue as you have begun … with all diligence. *"And we desire that every one of you do shew the same diligence to the full assurance of hope unto the end."* *(Hebrews 6:11).*

FALSE HOPE

The last barrier in your new walk is one that is more common than the church cares to admit. It is the greatest barrier of them all because, unless it is overcome, there will never be any sense of the blessed assurance that the Christian seeks. It is a false hope born out of a false salvation. Many, many of the people in our churches today have never genuinely been saved. In fact, one prominent evangelist has estimated that over 50% of the members of Baptist churches are not even saved! Other leaders place the figure even higher! The phenomenon is not new. Jesus spoke of this in His Sermon on the Mount:

> *"Enter ye in at the strait gate: for wide is the*
> *gate, and broad is the way, that leadeth to*
> *destruction, and MANY there be which go in*
> *thereat … Not every one that saith unto me, Lord,*
> *Lord, shall enter into the kingdom of heaven; but*
> *he that doeth the will of my Father which is in*
> *heaven. MANY will say to me in that day, Lord,*
> *Lord, have we not prophesied in thy name? and in*
> *thy name have cast out devils? and in thy name*

done many wonderful works? And then will I
profess unto them, I never knew you: depart from
me, ye that work iniquity." (Matthew 7:13, 21-
23). [Emphasis added]

My wife, Sandra, and I had been married only a few months when she came to me and expressed doubts about her salvation. She was not sure she was saved. She had been reared in a godly home and had hardly missed a day of church in her entire life. She had heard the greatest preachers in the world and attended a Bible college. How well I remember kneeling beside our bed with an open Bible and reading the wonderful plan of salvation together. We held hands and prayed and Sandra got the full assurance for which she so longed.

A man in our church came to my study for an appointment. As we began to talk, he began to tremble and to cry. "Pastor," he sobbed, "I am not sure that I am really saved. I have been plagued by doubts and I must find an answer to this!" I shared some scriptures with him and he prayed the sweetest childlike prayer I had ever heard from an adult man. He arose from his knees with the joy of Jesus upon his face. He was a changed man. He had found Christ for the first time, even though he had been in church for years. The next Sunday he came forward in the church service to make his decision public. After he had testified of his new-found faith, I discovered that there were others in our church with the same uncertainty and doubt. Within three months nineteen of our faithful church members had guinely trusted Christ as Saviour for the first time.

If you are struggling with doubts, as these did, and you do

not feel that it is because of the other factors we have mentioned, perhaps your doubt is given to you by the Holy Spirit for a reason. Someone has wisely said, "Doubt is to the human spirit what pain is to the human body ... it is a signal that something is wrong and needs attention." Recently I witnessed the interview of a prominent heart surgeon. I was especially interested in his comments because I had been experiencing some chest pains. I was jolted to hear him say, "Anytime a man over forty experiences any pain from his belly button to his collar bone, he had better get it checked out!" Needless to say, I beat a hasty path to my doctor for a check up. I endured a stress test and an EKG with good results and a newfound peace of mind. If the doubts persist, you should seek out a spiritual heart doctor, your pastor, for some counsel and prayer. He is given to you of God to help you through times such as this.

FIGHTING FOE

Hundreds of years ago the great Martin Luther penned these words to one of the greatest classics in the history of Christian music:

> A mighty fortress is our God,
> A bulwark never failing;
> Our helper He amid the flood
> Of mortal ills prevailing.
> For still our ancient foe
> Doth seek to work us woe-
> His craft and pow'r are great,
> And, armed with cruel hate,
> On earth is not his equal.
>
> Martin Luther, 1527-1529

Luther was right when he referred to our "ancient foe" who "doth seek to work us woe." This was a direct reference to the enemy of our soul, Satan. I introduce you to him with fear and trembling, for I abhor the thought of giving him any undue attention.

But the alternative of inattention is no less abhorrent. In fact, the Bible warns us about being *"ignorant of his devices."* *(2 Corinthians 2:11).* It is not my intention to present an exhaustive study of the doctrine of the devil, but merely to make you aware of his existence and his goal of attacking you. You see, before you became a Christian, you were not a threat to him because you basically did his bidding without knowing it (Ephesians 2:1-3.) But now that you have accepted Christ, you have a very real adversary. Therefore, *"Be sober, be vigilant; because your adversary the devil, as a roaring lion, walketh about, seeking whom he may devour." (1 Peter 5:8).*

He knows that he can no longer touch your eternal life; he has forever lost the chance to drag you down to hell. But he fears your influence upon others. He doesn't want you to win others to Christ or even to enjoy your life. So he will attack you to hinder your service to Christ. What can you do? *"Submit yourselves therefore to God. Resist the devil, and he will flee from you." (James 4:7).*

First and foremost, be certain that you are yielded to God in every area of your life. Then resist the devil. For fuller information about this element of the Christian life, see your pastor for his counsel and advice and read my book *"Living Purely in An Impure World."* But the basic goal of the devil is to get you, and the control of you he desires is in the realm of the mind. He is the *"father of **all** lies" cf. John 8:44* [Emphasis added] and desires to get you to believe his lies over the truth of God's Word. It is vital, then, that you know the Bible to enable you to resist his attacks on your mind. This is what the Lord Jesus used in Matthew chapter four. Each time Satan suggested something to Him, Christ referred to scriptures and said, *It is written,"* and then quoted a Bible passage to offset Satan's lie. Study this passage carefully and learn to emulate Christ's method of resisting the devil.

There is no question that Satan is a formidable foe, but you now have a power which is far greater than his. *"Ye are of God, little children, and have overcome them: because greater is he that is in you, than he that is in the world." (1 John 4:4).*

What a profound truth! You are of God now, you are His child, and His Holy Spirit dwells within you! That is the greatest power ever known in the universe and it is yours!

So you have no need to fear. Yes, the enemy is strong, but Christ is stronger! As Luther continues his great hymn, he reminds us,

Did we in our own strength confide
Our striving would be losing,
Were not the right Man on our side,
The Man of God's own choosing.
Dost ask who that may be?
Christ Jesus, it is He;
Lord Sabaoth His name,
From age to age the same;
And He must win the battle.

Luther seems to warm up to his subject as his thoughts rise up to the heavenlies. He sees the danger, but he sees the victory, too!

> And tho this world, with devils filled,
> Should threaten to undo us,
> We will not fear, for God hath willed
> His truth to triumph thru us.
> The prince of darkness grim —
> We tremble not for him;
> His rage we can endure,
> For lo! his doom is sure —
> One little word shall fell him.

I once heard of a man who claimed to sleep with two men every night: one was called Mr. Want To and the other was Mr. Have To. One morning he was awakened by a sharp pain in his side, only to discover that Mr. Have To was jabbing him with his elbow. "Get up!" he demanded. "You have to read your Bible and pray to start the day!" The man rolled over to get a little more sleep when he felt the pain again. "Get up!" All this commotion awakened Mr. Want To who was sleeping on the other side of the man, and he spoke up. "We don't want to!" "It doesn't matter; you have to," declared Mr. Have To.

An argument ensued, and the man, concluding that he wasn't going to get any more sleep anyway, resignedly got out of bed. He looked down to see Mr. Want To pulling the covers up around his chin and snuggling down into the covers. "Aren't you coming with us?" he asked. "I don't want to," was the reply. "Does he have to?" asked Mr. Have To.

The man took his Bible and, joined by Mr. Have To, plodded sluggishly down the hallway into the den. He turned the light on and, with Mr. Have To's help, began to read. After a bit the door cracked open and guess who was peeking in? You guessed it — Mr. Want To. "Can I join you?" he asked. "Does he have to?" asked Mr. Have To. "I want to!" said Mr. Want To. In short order the man, along with Mr. Have To and Mr. Want To, were having the best time in their devotions they had ever had!

And so, dear reader, these are the very real and present barriers to your new life in Christ. A false reliance upon feelings, the negative influence of ungodly friends, a confusion about fellowship with God vs. a relationship with God, forgetfulness or neglect, a false hope and a fighting foe. Understanding their existence and being prepared to recognize them will enable you to conquer them and continue on your journey with God.

Footnotes

[1] Ironside, H.A., *Full Assurance, New York: Loizeaux Brothers, Inc., 1937, p. 30.*

[2] Ibid, p. 42-45.

[3] Sweeting, George, *The Basics of the Christian Life,* Chicago: Moody Press, 1983, p. 108-109.

[4] Henry, Matthew, *Matthew Henry's Commentary, Vol. III,* New York: Fleming H. Revell Co., p. 920-921.

[5] Ironside, H.A., *First Epistle to the Corinthians*, Neptune: Loizeaux Brothers, p. 170.

[6] Vine, William E., *Vine's Concise Dictionary of the Bible*, Nashville: Thomas Nelson, Inc, p. 303.

∞ ∞ *Chapter Three* ∞ ∞

"Blessed Assurance"

The barriers discussed in the last chapter are real and operative in our lives. They will rob us of the joy of our salvation and they will produce "Blasted Assurance."

But just as there are barriers to our assurance, there are reliable sources to which we can turn for help to overcome them. They promise us the joy of "Blessed Assurance." These sources are the Word of God, the witness of the Spirit, and the works of our lives. Let's look at them closely.

THE WORD OF GOD

The prophet Hosea recorded a sad commentary about the people of Israel. *"My people are destroyed for lack of knowledge ..." (Hosea 4:6).*

God gives us all the knowledge we need for our Christian lives in the Word of God. It is a complete library to meet every need that we could possibly encounter. When we take our eyes off the Word, however, and look to other sources for help, we begin to fail in the knowledge of the Word; and eventually we will be destroyed. It is the Word of God, the Bible, that keeps us from sin. *"Thy Word have I hid in mine heart, that I might not sin against thee." (Psalm 119:11).*

Dr. John R. Rice recalls the problems he encountered as a young Christian because he failed to rely upon the inspired Word of God.

"When I was nine years old I trusted Christ as my Saviour. It was after a good sermon by a godly pastor in Gainesville, Texas. He preached upon the parable of the prodigal son and told us how any poor sinner who would turn to the Lord would receive a glad welcome and forgiveness and peace; and that, like the prodigal son, we would receive all these blessings without money and without price, wholly undeserving. Then he asked those who would take Christ as Saviour and trust Him, turning in their hearts to the Father's house for mercy and forgiveness, to come forward. I slid off the pew, walked down the aisle and took the pastor's hand to claim Christ as my Saviour. They did not take time to teach me any of the Word of God. Perhaps they thought I was too young. I went home so happy that day and asked my father if it would be alright for me to join the church and be baptized since I was now a Christian. He said, 'Well, son, when you are old enough to know you are a sinner and honestly repent of your sins and be regenerated, then it will be time enough to join the church.'

"I sat stricken and silent before my father. I did not know what all those big words meant – repentance, regeneration and more. I simply knew my father did not think I was saved! Well, I thought, my father was the wisest man in the world and a preacher besides; and if he thought I was not saved, I supposed I was not. Sadly I gave up the idea of joining the church and hoped the time would come when I would be old enough to be saved so my father would know that I was saved.

"The next morning on the way to school, I stopped under a willow tree down on Pecan Creek and prayed. I asked God to help me to be a good boy and asked Him to save other people since my father thought I was too young to be saved.

"I wish I could tell you all the sadness and disappointment of the next three years, ... We moved out to a ranch in west Texas and then to a little cow town. The company was not always the best. My mother had gone to Heaven and I was a motherless boy. I did not get much instruction in the Word of God. I got no assurance about salvation. Again and again I prayed for God to save me. Once I asked a godly preacher to pray for me and he asked me to pray for myself. So that night when I went home from the little church, I went out into the horses' stall and knelt down and asked God to forgive my sins and save me. I felt no change. I did not have any glorious experience. I did not see any light shining around about me. I did not hear the flutter of angel wings. No electricity came in at my head or went out at my fingers and toes! So I sadly went to bed without any assurance of salvation. Then I thought, 'Well, I had better settle this thing for good some way or other; so I got out of bed and prayed again. There on my knees I thought how strange it was, then when I realized I was a sinner and that there was nothing I could do to earn salvation and when God had promised so plainly that He would save people and that Jesus had died to pay for our sins – how strange, I thought, that God would not save me! I decided I would leave the matter in the hands of God the best I knew how and go to bed.

"I offered myself for membership in the church. I could not feel any great conviction for sin, and yet I did not know that I was saved. When, in that little west Texas church, they asked me to stand and give my "experience" and give my testimony before being received into the church, I simply said that I had thought about the matter a great deal, that I did not want to be a Methodist, so I had decided to be a Baptist! I was a trembling, inexperienced boy, twelve years old. I was frightened at speaking before the people. And they some way had more confidence in my salvation than my testimony would have warranted and received me in the church as a candidate for baptism!

"When I was baptized, I was strangely happy. Even yet, I could give no clear testimony as to when I was saved or how. Oh, I wished that I knew just how and when I was saved and could know for sure that it was settled for good! But when others gave the very date and place when they were saved and told how happy they had been, I could not give any such experience.

"Then, one glad day I began reading the New Testament and came upon those wonderful promises in the Gospel of John, like clusters of ripe fruit on a beautiful tree! *"As many as received him, to them gave he power to* *become the sons of God, **even to them that believe on his name.**" (John 1:12). "He that believeth on the Son hath everlasting life." (John 3:36). "Verily, verily, I say unto you, he that heareth my word, and believeth on him that sent me, hath everlasting life, and shall not come into condemnation; but is passed from death unto life." (John 5:24).*

"Oh, that last wonderful promise! I found that when I heard the Word of God and put my trust in the God who had sent His Son to save me, I then and there received everlasting life. I had often tried to remember that incident or that experience when I was nine years old and came to claim the Saviour publicly. I could not remember how I felt. I wondered if I had been as deeply moved as one must be to be saved. I recalled that a twelve-year-old boy who came the same day had been weeping and I had shed not a tear! I had thought many a time, if I were really saved, I would not do some of the things I do. But now I saw, praise the Lord, that when I had put my trust in Jesus Christ, then and there I received everlasting life! My doubts and fears were gone, gone, thank God, forever! From that day to this, I have never doubted for a moment that I am God's child. I know one thing beyond any doubt. When I trusted Jesus, depended on Him to forgive me, He did! The Word of God says so and that makes it so. On those promises I have hung the eternal welfare of my soul, and how sure, how unchanging is that blessed foundation for my faith!"[1]

How desperately every believer needs something firm and true upon which to hang the eternal welfare of his soul. And, thank God, we have it, the written Word of a Holy and righteous God! Hear what God says. *"And this is the record, that God hath given to us eternal life, and this life is in His Son. He that hath the Son hath life; and he that hath not the Son of God hath not life. These things have I written unto you that believe on the name of the Son of God; that ye may know that ye have eternal life ..." (1 John 5:11-13).*

The Apostle John places a great emphasis on the written record, and well he should. He says *"this is the record," "these things have I written ... that ye may know,"* and in the Gospel of John he reinforces this when he refers to the miracles recorded in that blessed book, *"... these are written, that ye might believe that Jesus is the Christ, the Son of God; and that believing ye might have life through his name." (John 20:31).*

Like John, the other apostles and other New Testament Christians shared a strong assurance about their salvation in Christ. Even the most casual perusal of the New Testament will reveal that one of the most striking characteristics of the apostles and the entire apostolic church was the element of certainty. These were men who knew. They didn't hope, they didn't wish – they knew. They knew their sins were forgiven; and they knew they had received eternal life. They knew beyond all doubt that they were on their way to Heaven.

Today many find this to be the most startling fact on the pages of the New Testament. And yet we read that they said, *"We know that we have passed from death unto life." (1 John 3:14);*

"We know that we are of God." (1 John 5:19); "We know in whom we have ... the forgiveness of sins." (Ephesians 1:7); "We know that, when he shall appear, we shall be like him." (1 John 3:2).

"We know that we know! Affirmation piled on top of affirmation! They not only knew, but they knew that they knew! It was this certainty, this unshakable faith, that enabled the apostles to withstand every difficulty, to overcome every obstacle, and to turn the world right side up for Jesus Christ. This was no mere vain boast but a ringing, glorious affirmation of faith in Jesus Christ; a stirring testimony to the risen Lord Jesus."[2]

This was the faith of our Christian forefathers. And what was the basis of such conviction? The Word of God!

How much better it is to rely on that which emanates from God than that which originates with man. Peter alluded to this when he described the process whereby we received the Word of God through human writers. He described some unusual experiences enjoyed in his life. He was an eyewitness to the glory of Christ and he heard the very voice of God on the Mount of Transfiguration. Imagine that! Beyond that, Peter had walked on the water, witnessed numerous miracles, sat at Jesus' feet, and performed miracles himself!

But Peter said that there was something better than all these things for the Christian life! What could be better than miracles such as these? "We have ... a **more sure word!** " More sure than the sight of Jesus transfigured in all His glory? More sure than miracles? What could be more sure than these? "We have ... a **more sure word of prophecy** ..." *cf. 2 Peter 1:19.*

[Emphasis added] Peter is saying that we have an instrument of instruction better than any experience … it is given by the Holy Spirit and recorded by men! This Word originated with God, was given to men by the Holy Spirit, and was written by them for our benefit. *"Knowing this first, that no prophecy of the scripture is of any private interpretation. For the prophecy came not in old time by the will of man: but holy men of God spake as they were moved by the Holy Ghost." (2 Peter 1:20-21).*

Far better than anything else is the written Word of God, written by men, given by the Holy Spirit. This record, called the Bible, is so reliable that Peter wrote that we need to follow it carefully. *"… whereunto ye do well that ye take heed, as unto a light that shineth in a dark place …" (2 Peter 1:19).*

One man vividly illustrates the importance of taking heed to the Scriptures. "I had rather have what this Bible says for the assurance of my salvation than to have every angel from Heaven come down to earth and tell me I am saved.

"Gabriel comes down from heaven. I say, 'Gabe, glad to have you here today. Is there anything you want to tell us?'

"He says, 'Yes, … , I want to talk to you.'

"Oh, what do you want to tell me!

"…, I want to tell you that you are saved, that you have everlasting life, and when you die you are going to Heaven.

"I say now Gabriel, I am glad you came. That is a

long trip for you to make, and I appreciate your coming. But you know, you didn't need to come. As a matter of fact, I have something better than your testimony.

"Oh, but I am an angel.

"I know you are an angel. But there is a group of angels who kept not their first estate but left their own habitation, and God hath reserved them in everlasting chains under darkness unto the judgment of the great day. You cannot always trust angels, Gabe.

"Listen, I had rather have the Bible than a tape recording of God's voice. I would play it on the tape recorder and hear, '[Christian], you are saved,' but I would always think some nut had put that on tape.

"I had rather have the written Word than have God call me on the telephone. If He called me on the phone and said, '[Christian], this is God. I want to tell you that you are saved,' I wouldn't believe it. You wouldn't either. You would think some nut had called you. You would never believe it was God.

"I would rather have this book than a telephone call from Heaven. I would rather have this Word than for the angels to come tell me I am saved. I am going to hang on to this. Boy, I like it!

"Why would I rather have this? Because this is what He gave me. 'These things have I written unto you that believe on the name of the Son of God; that ye may know that ye have eternal life ...'

"When you say, 'I hope I am saved' when you know you are trusting Jesus Christ, you are saying, 'I hope God told the truth.' You are implying that God could have lied about it.

"I am more sure that I am saved than I am that I am alive. I am more sure that I am saved than I am that I am married. I am more sure that I am saved than I am that I am on this platform. Why? I have better assurance for it. I have God Almighty's written Word that has never changed and never will change.

"A preacher once asked me, 'You mean the Bible is all you have for your assurance?' I said, 'Yes. Do you have anything better?' He thought a minute and replied, 'Well, I don't guess so.'

"Boy, you latch onto this and hang onto it. If everybody in town says, 'You are not saved. You just go to that old emotional church and that loud preacher hollers and tells you that you are saved. He has just sold you a false bill of goods,' down in your heart you say, 'no, it's not the loud preacher. It is God's Word, and I will stand on it.'"[3]

What authority there is in that blessed old Book! It is written to us from God and contains promises that we can believe despite contrary circumstances, emotions or witnesses.

A prisoner awaits the gas chamber on death row. It is only hours away now. His hands perspire, his stomach nauseates, and his mind rebels at the thought of death. But nothing can stop the movement of the hands on the clock outside his cell. It is inevitable ... there is no hope ... footsteps are heard approaching his cell. They are coming for him! NO! NO! It is too early! There is still a little time left for living! They can't take that from him! The door swings open and a piece of paper is thrust into his hand. He stiffens involuntarily at the sight of an outthrust hand. But wait! The hand holds a piece of paper... It feels crisp and new. It looks official with that seal upon it. He begins to read. One word stands out above all others p-a-r-d-o-n ... pardon ... PARDON ! ! ! It is a pardon from the Governor. Quickly now, ask him the question, "Have you been pardoned?" He nods his head. "Do you feel pardoned!" Still in the mindset of death, he has not yet fully grasped the enormity of his freedom. "Do you feel pardoned?" you repeat. He shakes his head from side to side. "If you don't feel pardoned, how do you know that you are?!" In mute amazement, he holds up the pardon, the written pardon. That's how he knows ... he has it in writing!!!

Far better than any feeling ... than any emotion ... than any circumstances is the promise in writing. How we need to thank God for His pardon. And, furthermore, we need to thank Him for not entrusting that pardon to our feelings or our circumstances. No, He put it in writing. He signed it. He sealed it with the Holy Spirit (Ephesians 1:13). I was in a prison of sin, I deserved to die to pay for my sins, but something wonderful happened ... I was pardoned! Paul explains it thusly, *"Blotting out the handwriting of ordinances that was against us, which was contrary to us, and took it out of the way, nailing it to his cross." (Colossians 2:14).* Some have described the "handwriting of ordinances" as "certificate of debt."

"This is a powerful word picture. In the day in which this

was written, the word translated as certificate of debt was widely known. Whenever a person would be convicted in a Roman court, a certificate of debt or bond would be prepared. The scribe of the court would itemize and write down every crime for which the person has been convicted. This certificate meant that the prisoner owed Caesar a prescribed payment for those crimes. It would then be taken with the prisoner to wherever he would be imprisoned and nailed to the door of his cell.

"What an illustration the Apostle Paul used to show how God has dealt with our sins. When Jesus hung on the cross nearly twenty centuries ago, that certificate of debt of every man who would ever live was nailed to the cross with Him.

"Our certificate of debt lists every time that we fall short of God's perfect law in thought, word or deed. Just as that certificate would have been nailed to the cell of the criminal, Jesus took our certificate of debt and nailed it to the cross.

"Why? Because He intended to pay for it.

"According to Roman law, when a person was put in prison and the certificate of debt was nailed to the door, it would remain there until the sentence was carried out. Then they would take this certificate and write across it the word meaning 'it is finished.' They would roll it up, give it to the prisoner, and he could never be punished for those crimes again.

"Did you know that was one of the last things Jesus shouted from the cross?

"Just before He bowed His head and said, 'Father, into Your hands I commit my spirit,' He gave a cry of victory. He called from the cross 'It is finished.' The Greek word for this is 'tetelestai,' meaning 'paid in full,' (John 19:30).

"Jesus took our certificate of debt and wrote across it in His own blood, 'Paid in Full.' We can never be tried for our sins again after we receive the pardon. It is settled forever in heaven by the blood of the only begotten Son of God.

"That's why it says in Colossians 2:14, 'He has taken it (our certificate of debt) out of the way, having nailed it to the cross.'"[4]

How do we know that we are pardoned? How do we know that God has forgiven us? How do we know that we are saved? … By our circumstances? By our feelings? No … because it is written … we have the decrees of God on this crucial matter in writing. How much better to rely upon that than upon our fickle feelings.

The first source of our Assurance is the written Word of God. Another is …

THE WITNESS OF THE SPIRIT

Ye have received the Spirit…the spirit itself beareth witness with our spirit, that we are the children of God: And if children, then heirs; heirs of God, and joint heirs with Christ." (Romans 8:15-17)

What a marvelous privilege to be children of God and heirs of God! We are informed of this by the Holy Spirit Himself whom we have received. We received Him the instant we trusted Christ as our Saviour, and He now makes His home in our hearts.

"Know ye not that ye are the temple of God, and that the Spirit of God dwelleth in you?" (1 Corinthians 3:16).

"... your body is the temple of the Holy Ghost [Holy Spirit] *which is in you, which we have of God, and ye are not your own!" (1 Corinthians 6:19).*

Think of it! As you read these words, the Holy Spirit of God dwells within you! As you go to work, He is there! As you sleep, He is there! As you walk, sit, or stand, He is there! In fact, He has promised that He will **never leave!!!** *"... he hath said, **I will never leave thee, nor forsake thee.**" (Hebrews 13:5).* [Emphasis added]

As He indwells, He ministers to us in several ways. He "opens our eyes to eternal values, lightens our minds to perceive the truth, fills our hearts with divine love, gives compassion for others, makes intercession for us when we know not how to pray, comforts in the hours of tears, strengthens in the midst of battle, lifts us in the vale of defeat."[5] But one of the most important ministries He provides for the convert who is young in the Lord is His ministry of assurance. He bears witness with us that we are really and truly His child.

THE WORKS OF OUR LIFE

Another source of our assurance is the works which we do with our lives. The Bible says that the very reason for which we were created is to accomplish good works. *"For we are his workmanship, created in Christ Jesus unto good works." (Ephesians 2:10).*

That is the reason for your existence, dear reader. God has a plan for you, a purpose to fulfill. That is the reason you were created. And in the fulfillment of that purpose you will find assurance that you are truly saved. A Christian who does nothing

74

for the Lord will eventually begin to doubt his salvation.

It is true that good works are the evidence of salvation and not the cause, but it is also true that your good works produce assurance in your heart. *"Commit thy works unto the Lord, and thy thoughts shall be established." (Proverbs 16:3).*

We should not wait until we are "moved by the Spirit" before attempting anything for God. Our labor for Christ is not predicated upon our feelings but upon obedience. If the Scriptures teach it, we should do it; and in the doing of it, we will find our hearts warmly touched.

What specific things can you do to strengthen the assurance in your own heart?

Walk It Out

Now that you are saved, you need to begin walking like a Christian. The first step you need to take is what is called a public profession of faith. This means that you should find a means of publicly announcing your commitment to Jesus Christ.

There are several ways that you can do that. You can take out a full page ad in the newspaper and in bold, four-inch letters print "**I HAVE BEEN SAVED!!**" and sign your name. Or you can rent a one-half ton flatbed truck, mount loudspeakers on the back and drive through your neighborhood, blaring forth your announcement: "ATTENTION PLEASE! THIS IS JOHN DOE! I GOT SAVED AND I WANT YOU TO KNOW ABOUT IT!" Then there is the opportunity of hiring a skywriter to fly over your city and imprint your testimony in the skies. (Of course, I am joking about these methods.)

No, the normal way of doing this is to attend a Bible-preaching church and, following the sermon, to respond to the public invitation to go forward and make known your decision. In our church and in many others, it is not required that you speak. The Pastor will announce to the congregation that you have trusted Christ as your Saviour. He will act as your mouth on your behalf.

Why go public? There are several reasons for this public testimony. First of all, there may be someone present who is thinking seriously about trusting Christ as Saviour. He is nervous about the prospect of going forward in front of all those people. Your example may be the very encouragement he needs. You could be the instrument of God to bring someone else to Christ. The Bible refers to this principle when it admonishes us to *"... consider one another to provoke unto love and to good works."* *(Hebrews 10:24).*

Secondly, there may be someone present who has also trusted Christ and is contemplating making it public. Your obedience could encourage him also.

And then, there are many Christians present in the service. How they rejoice when they see another soul added to their spiritual family! What a blessed event this is for everyone!

But one of the most important reasons to make your decision public is because God commands us to do it. *"For with the heart man believeth unto righteousness; and with the mouth confession is made unto salvation. For the scripture saith, Whosoever believeth on him shall not be ashamed."* *(Romans 10:10-11).* *"Whosoever therefore shall confess me before men, him will I confess also before my Father which is in heaven." (Matthew 10:32).*

76

God is not honored by the "silent witness" brand of Christianity. He calls for men and women, boys and girls, and young people to take a bold stand for Him. *"For the scripture saith, Whosoever believeth on him shall not be ashamed." (Romans 10:11).* It is no shame to be associated with the King of kings and Lord of lords. The world is not impressed with a faith that hides its light under a bushel! I like the song the Sunday school children sing, "This little light of mind, I'm gonna let it shine." And why? Why does God ask us to let it shine? *"Let your light so shine before men that they may see your good works, and glorify your Father which is in heaven." (Matthew 5:16).*

The act of making your decision public directly impacts your sense of assurance. Your "thoughts are established" when you take this stand for Christ. You are now committed. The word is out now, and this knowledge will prevent you from going back to the old crowd and the old lifestyle. Keep the news to yourself and the time will come when you will be tempted to sin because no one knows about your decision. But now everyone knows! When you identify yourself with Christ and His crowd, the very act of doing it will reinforce the assurance of your heart.

Write It Out

Open your Bible and turn to the flyleaf in the front. Take your pen and write the date, time and circumstances of your salvation. Write something like this: "I was saved on (date) in my home. I was led to Christ by (person). I hereby commit my life to the Lord Jesus Christ and will live for Him." Signed: (your signature). This simple statement will mean much to you in the years ahead. I know many Christians who regret that they did not make a record of the most important date of their lives.

After you have done this, you should write out your personal testimony. A testimony is simply a statement of what has happened in your life … what Christ has done for you. This should be similar to the statement of commitment in your Bible, but it will be in much more detail. Write out the circumstances of your experience, how God brought you to the place of surrender, what event God used to touch your heart, etc. perhaps a sermon, a song, a prayer, another person's love and concern, etc. Be positive and forward-looking rather than backward-looking. Be careful not to glorify your sin. I have heard many testimonies that went into such detail about the sinful past that I felt I could never have a good testimony unless I had stolen, murdered or been in prison. Give God all the glory. Tell where you were, who you were with, the words you prayed, etc. Write down everything you can remember and then take it to your pastor for him to read. After he has approved it, you need to …

Talk It Out

Take the opportunity to read it to everyone you can find who will listen: your Sunday school class, your family, your friends, the church congregation, etc. The more you read it to others, the more it will be reinforced into your heart and the more your "thoughts shall be established." This will help you, and it will also get the Gospel out to everyone who hears it. After you have done this, you will be prepared to give your testimony without your written paper before you.

The source of your assurance, dear reader, is three-fold. First and foremost is the **Word of God**. It is the standard of our lives, the basis of all our belief. Secondly, it is the **Witness of the**

Spirit. The precious Holy Spirit of God assures and reassures us that we are truly saved. Lastly is the **Works of Your Life**. If you will walk it out, write it out and talk it out, your "thoughts shall be established."

Footnotes

[1] Rice, John R., *Seven Secrets of a Happy, Prosperous Christian Life,* Murfreesboro: Sword of the Lord Press, 1949, p. 12-15.

[2] Hutson, Curtis, *Building and Battling*, Murfreesboro: Sword of the Lord Press, 1974, p. 68-70.

[3] Ibid.

[4] Lindsey, Hal, *Satan Is Alive and Well on Planet Earth*, Grand Rapids: Zondervan Publishers, 1972, p. 201-203.

[5] Sweeting, p. 107.

✎ ✎ *Conclusion* ✎ ✎

I am so happy for you in your decision to trust Christ as your Saviour. You are now a part of the family of God, along with me and all the millions of people before you who have made the same decision.

It is with this family feeling in mind that the great Apostle John wrote to his converts like a father to his children. He refers to them as *"little children,"* and gave them some fatherly counsel. He wrote a lengthy letter to them which is part of the Bible. It is the epistle of 1 John and was written for an express purpose, a purpose that I understand and share with him in the writing of this book for you. *"These things have I written unto you that believe on the name of the Son of God;* **that ye may know that ye have eternal life***, and that ye may believe on the name of the Son of God." (1 John 5:13).* [Emphasis added]

It is for this reason that we carefully reviewed the steps you took in becoming a child of God and what you have as a result - *"that ye may know that ye have eternal life."*

It is for this reason that we discussed the enemies of your assurance; the things which produce "blasted assurance" - *"that ye may know that ye have eternal life."*

It is for this reason that we covered the great elements which make up the "blessed assurance" which are so needed in your new life *"that ye may know that ye have eternal life."*

My prayer for you is that the truths within these pages will help you to *"know that ye have eternal life,"* and that they will ground you in the strength of that conviction. Build your faith upon the Word of God and base your hope of heaven upon its promises. Such solid belief will hold you in good stead, even in the worst storms of your life.

In the midst of a horrible thunderstorm, a father became aware of a presence in his bedroom. Through the darkness he said, "Who is there?" "It's me Daddy," came the reply of his small daughter. "What are you doing out of bed, honey?" he asked. "I just wanted to be sure you were here," she replied. "I can sleep better if I know you are in the room next to me."

And so does the child of God sleep better when he knows that God is near. *"I will both lay me down in peace, and sleep; for thou, Lord, only makest me dwell in safety."* (Psalm 4:8).

It is heartening and assuring to know that your Heavenly Father is always near, even as near as your own heart, for that is where His Spirit resides with His child. What a joy to *"know that ye have eternal life."*

Cleaning Out the Cow Stall

How to Experience Absolute Forgiveness

While growing up on a farm in Indiana, it fell my lot to clean out the stall where we housed our cattle. This was a dreaded job because the cows, shall we say, were so productive. President Reagan, while speaking to the Canadian Parliament, alluded to the American economy as a baby, having "an insatiable appetite on one end, and a total lack of control on the other." Certainly the same can be said about cows.

Because laziness is often the mother of invention, I looked for a better way and found one. I learned that by merely covering the cow's "lack of control" with some fresh straw, I could effectively convince the casual onlooker that the stall was clean. I did not reckon on the lack of cooperation of the cows, however. They dumbly walked over the fresh straw, mashing it into their indiscretions. They would follow up on this with a new deposit whereupon I would lay down a fresh layer of straw, only to be followed by another deposit. After some uncounted days of this novel approach, I remember my father walking into the stall. He noticed that the ceiling of the stall was appreciably closer to the floor. After a close encounter of the worst kind (a euphemism for a spanking), I was instructed to get to work and not to leave the stall till I cleaned out every vestige of straw and manure. But over time, the odoriferous layers of pungent deposits had hardened into a thick, impenetrable carpet which defied the strength of Samson or the wisdom of Solomon. I tried a pitch fork, but one of its teeth broke off. I then used a pick-axe. It went in easily enough, but it wouldn't come out. I soon learned that the only way the deposits were going to come out was the same way they went down, a layer at a time. I had to use a spade and skim over a few inches at a time, moving slowly across the stall. But in time (very much time) I finally reached the dirt floor of the barn.

Unfortunately, such an approach is not confined to the cow stall. As a young Christian, I learned to deal with sin the same way. I would put off my sin, cover it up for appearances, and plan to deal with it later. I had not yet learned that *"He that covereth his sins shall not prosper." (Proverbs 28:13)*. I soon learned that this is a common practice for believers and a major reason for the lack of spiritual victory and joy. We are simply not thorough and effective in our dealings with personal sin. We cover them up.

Nowhere is this illustrated more clearly than in the life of King David. After committing adultery and murder, he ran from God for one full year. His great prayer recorded in Psalm 51 demonstrates not only the horrible consequences of his sin, but also a plan for dealing with it. First comes...

Conviction of Sin

During his period of backsliding, David had come under the powerful weight of guilt and conviction. A major source of his discomfort is revealed in 2 Samuel 12:1, *"And the Lord sent Nathan unto David ..."* He arrived with the story of a rich man who stole a cherished ewe lamb from a poor neighbor. When

David's anger was kindled against the rich man, Nathan said unto David, *"Thou art the man" (verse 7)*. Without a doubt, one of God's most effective arrows of conviction is the man of God whom He sends to the Christian. For this reason, He admonishes the preacher to *"Cry aloud, spare not, lift up thy voice like a trumpet, and shew my people their transgression ..." (Isaiah 58:1)*.

It is not enough for a man to speak his philosophies or ideas. It was Nathan's *"thus saith the Lord" (2 Samuel 12:7)* which gave him his authority. Thus we see the vital importance of preaching, teaching, and counseling with the all-powerful Word of God! It is *"quick and powerful and sharper than any two-edged sword; piercing even to the dividing asunder of soul and spirit and of the joints and marrow, and is a discerner of the thoughts and intents of the heart." (Hebrews 4:12)*.

The Christian has additional sources of conviction as well! There is the Spirit of God, which *"will reprove the world of sin" (John 16:8)*, and the child of God, who is to *"exhort one an-other daily lest ye be hardened through the deceitfulness of sin." (Hebrews 3:13)*.

In light of these multiple sources of conviction, how is it that David and lesser known saints manage to come to a place of spiritual hardness? An obvious conclusion is that they remove themselves from these influences. When there is coldness and backsliding, there is invariably a corresponding removal of one's self from the Man of God, the Word of God, the Spirit of God, and the child of God. The solution? It is seeking anew these sources of conviction and exposing your coldness to the spiritual warmth of their message, and then yielding to the truth they speak. Such a surrender in David's heart is evident by his memorable words, *"I have sinned."*

Confidence in God

Once David experienced the conviction of God, he immediately ran into the arms of God. He envisioned God's *"lovingkindness"* and the *"multitude"* of his *"tender mercies."* David's trusting view of a loving Heavenly Father provided the incentive to turn to Him for forgiveness.

I have asked many Christians and pastors over the years, "Do you feel that God loves you and accepts you as a person?" The answers have been astounding and amazingly uniform. Responses vary from doubt to outright denial, revealing a yawning chasm in the orthodoxy of fundamentalism in the form of a negative and destructive view of God. It is amazing how many other errors flow out of this single error in our thinking. Certainly one of these errors is a paralyzing reluctance to turn to God. Indeed, if you see God's arms sternly folded, you will not be as quick to run into them as the person who sees God with His arms fully extended. The father of the prodigal son, lovingly scanned the horizon for that first glimpse of his wayward child, and then ran pell-mell with robes flapping in the breeze and offered a "welcome home" embrace. Like him, the God of the Bible always has open arms for the penitent child.

One street-wise ghetto boy was invited for the first time to a Sunday school in his neighborhood. The lesson was from James 4:8, *"Draw nigh to God and he will draw nigh to you."* Upon his return home, his mother asked him, "What did you learn in church today?" He replied, "I learned that if you draw a knife on God, He'll draw a knife on you!" This is a humorous perception from the lips of a child of the streets, but it is tragic when it is found in the heart of a child of God.

Because of David's lofty view of God, he was drawn irresistibly into His arms. It was the *"goodness of God"* that led him to repentance (Romans 2:4).

Conscientiousness in Dealing with Sin

Because of David's wholesome and secure view of God, he was able to transparently open his soul to God's holy gaze. No effort was spared in dealing thoroughly with every vestige of sin. He did not use a flippant, "If I have sinned " approach, nor a general "Forgive me for all my sins" prayer. Rather he was specific about his sin.

He used three key words in his prayer to describe his wickedness — sin, iniquity, and transgression (verses 1-2).

Sin

The meaning of this word is seen in an archer drawing his bow and firing his arrow, but the arrow's trajectory loses momentum and falls short of its intended target. It means "to fall short," to "miss the mark," and is referred to by James, *"to him that knoweth to do good and doeth it not, to him it is sin". (James 4:17).* It is commonly called the sin of omission. David knew to do good and failed to do so; *"at a time when kings go forth to battle...David tarried at Jerusalem." (2 Samuel 11:1).* A small act of neglect to some, but David saw it differently. He saw his sin as "exceeding sinful" to the point that he pled with God to "cleanse" him of its vile influence.

Before David committed adultery, he simply failed to do his duty. Before the believer is steeped in gross immorality, he will generally neglect the little things so vital to his fellowship with God: his Bible reading, daily prayer, witnessing, giving, serving, church attendance, etc. Any neglect in these areas portend worse things to come. If David had dealt severely with sin, he would not have committed...

Iniquity

Iniquity is a sin of commission which results in further iniquities. At each step, a conscious step is taken, but generally with little thought to the past or future. It is the gratification of the present which allures the sinner here. Isaiah wrote about this phenomenon when he said, *"All we like sheep have gone astray; we have turned every one to his own way." (Isaiah 53:6).* He labels this activity as "iniquity." The picture here is of a foolish sheep who sins by degrees; and with each mindless choice, he finds himself drawn further and further from the Shepherd. He buries his nose in a moist, succulent morsel of grass, relishing the scent and savoring the taste while thinking of nothing but the immediate satiation of his boundless appetite. While enjoying his treat, his eye is drawn to more tempting fare just inches away. Although it is the opposite direction of the Shepherd, its distance is so miniscule that he gives it no thought. He responds reflexively to his impulses only to find yet another morsel even farther away. This process continues until the witless sheep suddenly discovers that the Shepherd is nowhere to be found. He is lost! He has "gone astray!"

David loafed when he should have been working, then his eyes fell on the appealing morsel of a lovely woman. He looked at her and then his look led to the commitment of iniquity — first by sending for her, then talking with her, then the unthinkable lapse of righteousness followed by lying to cover his sin. Each step was a deliberate choice to sin with little thought to the future. Most likely, when David tarried in Jerusalem he had no plans to commit adultery, but one iniquity led to another until the sheep was lost. David confessed his iniquity, pleading with God to go deep in His cleansing and to *"wash me throughly from mine iniquity." (Psalm 51:2).* His iniquity led him to...

Transgression

Unlike a gradual departure from God by degrees, this step involves full knowledge of the consequences, absolute rejection of God's authority, and a deliberate choice to commit spiritual suicide despite the outcome...all for the sake of feeling good. David stood poised on the brink of the abyss of sin and studied the boiling caldron of wickedness before him. For a brief instance, his senses rebelled against the noxious fumes. But from within its sulfuric depths came a siren's song, a melodic invitation to forbidden pleasures. Throwing caution to the winds, he plunged in. At first the experience was sweet, but it quickly soured when he came to his senses. Upon hearing the news of Bathsheba's pregnancy, he impulsively attempted to cover his tracks which led to the murder of Uriah. The unspeakable had happened! David had committed transgression, a crime so heinous that mere washing was not enough; he pled with God to blot it out.

In all this, David was painfully honest, brutally transparent, and conscientious in his admission of guilt. He did not avoid the painful reality of vivid introspection; he welcomed it as a necessary step toward...

Confession of Sin

David's sin was against God *"against thee and thee only have I sinned." (Psalm 51:4)*. For twelve long months he had not been honest with Him about the severity of his sin. He knew that God desired *"truth in the inward parts," (Psalm 51:6)* and David knew he had not been forthright with God in his estimate of his sinfulness.

When I was a new Christian, I was directed to read the epistle of 1 John. What joy flooded my soul when I first discovered the truth of 1 John 1:9: *"If we confess our sins, he is faithful and just to forgive us our sins and to cleanse us from all unrighteousness."* I assumed that *"confess"* meant to list any sins and so I did. I thought it meant to admit I did wrong so I did that. Confession includes these things but even more. The original word homologeo, (homo = "together with") (logeo = "thoughtful word or speech"), means to speak together with or say the same thing as another. In confession we are to say the same thing about our sins that God does; we are to think with the mind of Christ and feel with the heart of God the sense of awfulness that He feels at the tragedy of our sins. This is foreign to human nature. We are prone to cover our sins. We want to minimize their impact and deny their heinousness.

An example of this is the new vocabulary we have acquired in our culture. We have softened our view of sin by our unwillingness to agree with God about it. For example, we have substituted dysfunction for sin, disease for drunkenness, gay for sodomy, success motivation for greed, and self-esteem for self-centeredness. We no longer say that a person is guilty of fornication, he is sexually active. He did not commit rape - merely sexual misconduct. There is no murder of unborn children, only abortion, or better yet, pro-choice. Of course, none of this is our fault; we are not sinners but victims.

God's view is far different. He describes our sin with such words as "vomit," "abominable," and "vile." He likens our sinfulness to leprosy and even our righteousness to filthy rags. True confession, then, is facing God's *"truth in the inward parts,"* to know wisdom in the *"hidden part"* of man, to say about sin what God says. So David said, *"I acknowledge my transgressions."* And the result of this bone-jarring transparency?...

Cleansing of Sin

David pled with God to *"wash me throughly"*—not thoroughly, but throughly. The picture here is a deep inner cleansing. I read about a new soap different from conventional soaps; it has an active enzyme which attacks the dirt within the fibers of cloth. It goes beyond a mere superficial cleaning and burrows deep within the fabric. This is the cleansing David desired and received. It is the same cleansing that the blood of Christ provides every repentant sinner. *"The blood of Jesus Christ ... cleanseth us from all sin." (1 John 1:7b).* It is vital to understand that David's cleansing was the result of a careful, Spirit-led process, not merely lip service to God; but even then, David did not stop. He did not seek forgiveness merely to revel in its attendant feelings. He sought to be used of God. He took the next vital step required in any process of thorough restoration.

Consecration to Service

David committed himself to salvaging transgressors, soul winning, singing God's praises, serving again as king, and even sacrificing to his God (verses 12-19). In other words, he consecrated himself anew to the service of God which he had previously abandoned. The effect of this step was to reinforce his commitment and seal his decision. He began to live out his new-found freedom.

It is never enough for the well-meaning Christian merely to make a decision at the altar without the added dimension of consecration. Much Sunday evening sincerity is lost in Monday morning ambivalence. The wise counselor will direct the seeker to confirm his decision through active service to God. This step resulted in David's ...

Continuation of Usefulness

Despite David's sin and its subsequent pain, (and oh, the pain he suffered!), he was still used of God. In fact, history reveals that of the 73 Psalms David wrote, 42 were written after his infamous sin. His newly restored fellowship with God was evident in his renewed walk. Truly the Master Potter took a marred vessel and *"made it again another vessel, as seemed good to the potter to make it." (Jeremiah 18:4)*. Surely Solomon was right when he wrote, *"Better is the end of a thing than the beginning thereof." (Ecclesiastes 7:8)*. The key to David's usefulness was his steps to forgiveness and his determined commitment to do God's will.

A man was once being trained to be a football scout. He attended a game with his trainer; and hoping to impress him, he began pointing out potential players. He watched one boy get hit, stay down, and be carried off the field. "We don't want that guy, do we?," he asked. He watched another get knocked down, get up, get knocked down again, and then stay down. He, too, was carried off the field. "We don't want that guy either, do we?," he announced. But one boy got knocked down, got up, got knocked down again and got up repeatedly throughout the entire game. His uniform was torn and muddy and streaked with his own blood, but he wouldn't quit. "That's the guy we want isn't it!" he exclaimed. "No," said his trainer, "we want the guy knocking everybody down!" Too often, we pride ourselves for getting up, but the Christian life is more than that. It is more than merely refusing to be overcome; it is being an overcomer. *"Be not overcome of evil, but overcome evil with good." (Romans 12:21).*

Through some hard experiences, and David's example, I learned the importance of keeping the cow stall clean, not just the one in the barn but the one of the heart as well.

Getting to Know Us
L.E.A.D. Ministries
Crisis Counseling for Those in Ministry

Who We Are

Dr. Jim Binney has been a pastor, teacher, youth pastor, church planter, and executive administrator. He served as a pastor for 16 years in three churches and more recently served as Interim Pastor for Calvary Baptist Church in Simpsonville, SC. He knows well both the blessings and rigors of the ministry. He founded L.E.A.D. Ministries in 1989 when he came to Moorehead Manor with his wife Sandra. L.E.A.D.'s primary focus is ministering to Christian leaders who are now more than ever under the attack of Satan.

He has drawn upon the strength and grace of God to help these leaders in need; and he and his wife have ministered to hundreds of Christian leaders who have come for help in their week-long program of counseling and renewal. Although the location has moved from Ohio to South Carolina, the ministry has stayed focused on helping those who are in the forefront of the battle, those in full-time Christian service.

Our Mission

The primary goal of L.E.A.D. Ministries is to encourage pastors, deacons and other leaders in ministry, through biblical counseling.

Hundreds of leaders and their wives have come for counseling since 1989. After spending a week of counseling, many have seen broken marriages restored, some have received a renewed vision for their ministry, others have experienced victory over personal struggles, but all have clearly seen the value of Christ's counsel about taking time out from the ministry to gain a fresh perspective: *"And he said unto them, Come ye yourselves apart into a desert place, and rest a while: for there were many coming and going, and they had no leisure so much as to eat" (Mark 6:31).*

Dr. Binney's philosophy behind personal counseling is that the Bible is sufficient to address every need. The Word of God is central in restoring hope to the discouraged, in revealing misconceptions about God's expectations and in renewing relationships. That philosophy permeates every other facet of the ministry.

Testimonies

"The ONLY reason I am still in the ministry today is because you skillfully and lovingly applied the Word of God to my life and situation. Your book '*The Ministry of Marriage*' has made me the Christian husband I always wanted to be - **but didn't know how to be**! My wife and I are excited about the possibility of working on our marriage at one of your week-long sesions. You mean so much to me - I will spend the rest of my ministry making you glad that you invested your ministry in my life !!!"

Pastor, Florida

"Thank you for the renewed hope you have given us. We look forward to getting back in the ministry with His strength and His wisdom."

Pastor and Wife, Michigan

"Your counseling is accurate, penetrating and healing. It is a biblical 'bomb' and balm. You and Sandra are hand and glove. Thank you for holding us."

Assistant Pastor, Illinois

"You have made me feel so safe and accepted. It is significant to me that someone we've only just met could show such love and compassion. Thank you for never judging, even when the deepest secrets came out."

Pastor and Wife, California

APPENDIX